"Anna's work is straightforward and down-to-earth. Her book, like her workshops, gives practical, easy-to-use tips for looking your best so you can *be* your best."

> —*George Vukotich,*
> *Director of Leadership Development,*
> *HSBC*

"Anna remains an ongoing resource for me, providing insight and understanding that has been invaluable in my career and my daily life. There is no one like her."

> —*Connie DuBois,*
> *Director of Communications,*
> *Siemens Medical Diagnostics*

"This book is an excellent guide for professional and personal growth and a tool that can provide the road map for success. *Change One Thing* should be on everyone's must-read list!"

> —*Shelia C. Hill, President and CEO,*
> *Chicago Minority Business Development*
> *Council, Inc.*

"Anna Wildermuth is an expert on making change happen. She knows what it takes to develop a personal image— communication skills, organizational savvy, presentation style, and appearance—that reflects who you are *and* leads to success as a business professional. Following her practical and knowledgeable guidance will enable you to make personal change a reality."

> —*Nancy A. Newton, Ph.D.,*
> *Professor, Business Psychology,*
> *the Chicago School of Professional*
> *Psychology*

"Wildermuth is a professional who achieves dramatic results almost immediately. Through her seminars, our employees have gained a greater sense of self-esteem and confidence, and our company has enjoyed improved productivity and morale."

—*Ed Marinelli, President, Electri-Flex Co.*

"Do not underestimate the improvements in your personal image that just a few suggestions from Anna Wildermuth can provide. Even for accomplished speakers and presenters, her advice is extremely helpful, motivating, and right-on."

—*Michael P. Chu,*
Intellectual Property Attorney,
Former President, National Asian Pacific
American Bar Association, Chicago

"Anna made me believe I could be a successful presenter. I was concerned about my weight, but she convinced me to go with my strength, which is my sense of humor. As soon as I got my first laugh, I was hooked.

—*Sheryl Jedlinski,*
Motivational Speaker and Cofounder of
pdplan4life.com

CHANGE
ONE
THING

Discover What's Holding You Back and Fix It—with the Secrets of a Top Executive Image Consultant

Anna Soo Wildermuth with Jodie Gould

New York   Chicago   San Francisco   Lisbon   London   Madrid   Mexico City
Milan   New Delhi   San Juan   Seoul   Singapore   Sydney   Toronto

To my sisters, MeePhon, Mary, Julie, and Sue. To my oldest and dearest friend, Michael O'Malley. And to my son, Eric, and his family for their unconditional love and support.
AW

To my mother, Betty Gould, for all of her support and sage advice throughout the years. To Helen Katel for her heart and soul. And to my beloved husband, Robert Katel, and daughter, Samantha. Don't change a thing.
JG

1 2 3 4 5 6 7 8 9 10 11 12 13 14 15 16 17 18 19 20 21 22 23 24   FGR/FGR   0 9

ISBN   978-0-07-162435-0
MHID   0-07-162435-X

Interior design by Monica Baziuk

McGraw-Hill books are available at special quantity discounts to use as premiums and sales promotions or for use in corporate training programs. To contact a representative, please e-mail us at bulksales@mcgraw-hill.com.

This book is printed on acid-free paper.

CONTENTS

ACKNOWLEDGMENTS

▶▶ THERE ARE BOOKS in which you tell a story, and there are books in which you share whatever wisdom you hope you have accumulated over the years. As I write this book of the latter variety, virtually everyone with whom I have come into contact has made some sort of contribution.

There are, however, a few who must be acknowledged by name. First is the group of long-time supporters who have provided me with unconditional encouragement for every venture I have undertaken. Ron Jedlinski, Tony and Sheryl Jedlinski, Bill Bridgman, Brian Little, Connie DuBois, and Tim Chapman have "been there for me" no matter what the circumstances.

My corporate clients have shown me that learning is a two-way street. Among those to whom I am especially thankful for these synergistic opportunities are the individuals I have worked with at HSBC, Allstate, Harris Bank, and McDonald's.

My colleagues at the Association of Image Consultants International have grown with me both personally and professionally over the past twenty years. Particular appreciation goes to Lynne Henderson Marks, Helena Chenn, Marion Gellatly, and Bev Dwane.

Thanks also to the members of my Toastmasters chapter who showed up two Mondays every month at 7 A.M. sharp to give me all kinds of communications pointers and coaching ideas.

And, finally, I am indebted to those who believed in this book and joined me in bringing it to fruition: my agent, Linda Konner; my co-writer, Jodie Gould; and our editor, Emily Carlson, and copyeditor, Karen Schenkenfelder.

—Anna Wildermuth

To my friend and superagent Linda Konner for her tireless efforts on my behalf. My thanks to Anna for bringing me onto to this project, and to all the McGraw-Hill editing, production, and marketing people who have had a hand in this book.

—Jodie Gould

INTRODUCTION

▶▶ ARE YOU STUCK in a dead-end job? Afraid of being demoted or laid off due to cutbacks? Are you not getting the kind of recognition or attention you deserve at work or in your personal life? In my twenty-plus years as an image consultant working with hundreds of men and women, including celebrities, politicians, and top executives from Fortune 500 companies, I've met too many people who are afraid to make a change. The reluctance to shake things up can be paralyzing, which is why so many people stay in an unhappy job, marriage, or relationship. As dissatisfied as we may feel, the same old same old is far more comfortable than going in a new, unfamiliar direction.

This book is for anyone who wants to make a change but doesn't know where to begin. It will help you take that first step toward turning your life around, starting with one simple change. Whether you need to fix your hair, posture, attitude, or diction, I will help you overcome the obstacles that prevent you from achieving true success. Not everything will be solved overnight—sometimes therapy is an important part of getting to the core of your problems—but as an image consultant and coach, I can work from the outside in to help change the way you think about yourself and, by extension, the way others perceive you. This simple step can work wonders to improve your situation.

Ask yourself this question: If you could change one thing about yourself, what would it be? Do you have an old-fashioned, tired look? A defeatist attitude ("I'm too old, too young, too inexperienced")? Whatever is holding you back, the advice in this book will help you discover why you are not where you want to be and will show you how to start the process of transformation.

I will share the tips that I give in my private sessions and workshops, starting with Chapter 1's description of the ten most common self-sabotaging excuses people make and how to overcome them. Next, each of the following chapters begins with a self-assessment quiz that will allow you to pinpoint your weaknesses. Each chapter then offers advice that will help you fix your problem areas.

One of my clients, a female astronaut, complained that she wasn't getting enough respect from her male colleagues. She was smart, pretty, and good at her job, so her problem wasn't a lack of confidence. Rather, she felt her looks kept men from taking her seriously. I didn't want to make her less attractive, so I had to find another way of winning her fellow astronauts' admiration. I discovered that she could be dictatorial in meetings, which is not the best strategy when you're working with men who don't like to be told what to do. I told her she needed to suggest, not tell. Instead of saying, "Do it this way," she should say, "Have you considered doing it this way?" or "May I make a suggestion?" The strategy worked, and she was accepted into the aerospace fraternity.

Similarly, a young receptionist who worked in a financial institution came to me because she felt that her coworkers didn't take her seriously. She had a bubbly personality, which made her well liked, but she often came to work wearing black leather jackets. It was a good look for a nightclub but not right for a conservative corporate environment. When she traded in the leather for a tailored suit jacket, people started to look at her differently. She was eventually promoted from receptionist to bank officer. I told her she didn't have to give up expressing herself; she could add a beaded necklace or other fun accessory. It was that simple.

This book offers an array of wardrobe styles to choose from, based on your body shape, height, complexion, and field of work. And along with knowing the right thing to wear, it's just as important to know the proper etiquette and basic business protocols for working, socializing after hours, and traveling abroad. I will give you tips for changing your business image, body image, and general self-image, as well as strengthening your communication and interviewing skills. In this turbulent and highly competitive business climate, it's essential that you put your best image forward.

The Beautiful Swan

My parents, who were born and raised in China, had five daughters. The fact that we were all girls was an enormous disappointment to our parents, because in Chinese culture, it is imperative to have a boy to carry on the family lineage. My parents felt that I, as the oldest, should have been a boy.

We were the only working-class Asian family in a wealthy suburb of Chicago. We had moved there from the inner city because my mother wanted her kids to go to a better school. My father owned a laundry, but the property in which he had invested our family savings was torn down to make room for a highway. After that, life was a struggle. All seven of us lived in one small room behind the new laundry my father bought, while the people I went to school with lived in large houses and vacationed in Florida or Europe.

My Cantonese name is Soo Phon, which means "Beautiful Swan." I was proud of that name when I was a young girl, but on my first day of school, the nuns made me change it to Anna because Soo Phon sounded "too foreign."

When I was six years old, I lost 60 percent of my hearing in both ears, a condition I inherited from my hearing-impaired father. Fortunately for me, my last name was Chin, so by the alphabetical standard, I was usually selected to sit in the front of the class. I learned how to read lips in order to get through school, but I was rarely invited to do things with the other children because I couldn't hear what was going on. I was able to get by with only lip reading until I got married and had a baby, when I needed a hearing aid to hear my son crying.

In high school, I belonged to a girls' athletic association. We weren't the most popular group in the school, but we were smart and good at sports. One day when my sisters and I were all sitting around the dinner table, I asked who the group's new president was. They all looked at me as if I had grown an extra head. "You don't know?" they said incredulously. "You are!" I hadn't gotten the official call yet. Being the head of this association helped me live up to my Chinese name–I felt more like Beautiful Swan, less like the ugly duckling.

My first real career out of college was as a real estate agent, and let me tell you, I stank at it. I couldn't sell water to a fish. In my first year, I earned just $117.42. If it weren't for my husband, I would have starved. I talked too fast, had a horribly big perm, and wore a ring on every finger and long, flowing skirts. Nobody could figure me out. I knew I had to do something differently if I wanted to be successful. I decided to study the people in my office who were making money. I was young and at first thought

I knew everything, but it was clear that I needed to start learning from my successful coworkers.

I soon realized how crucial it is to make a good impression in the first sixty seconds. I knew I needed to change my image. First, I cut my hair and let it go natural again. When that got a positive reaction from my coworkers, I went one step further and got rid of my jewelry. Next, I shortened my skirts and put on jackets. By the time I left real estate to become an image consultant in 1986, I had sold $3.5 million in property and had become a lifetime member of the Two Million Dollar Club.

Although I was a successful agent, I knew deep down that selling real estate wasn't what I was meant to do. I had always enjoyed making my friends over, turning *them* into beautiful swans, and I was good at it. So I researched the field, joined the industry associations, and eventually got the proper accreditation to open Personal Images, Inc. Today my corporate clients include Allstate Insurance Company, McDonald's Corporation, and General Electric. Once again, I rose to the top of my profession because I was willing to change. I was able to overcome the low expectations of my parents and my colleagues in order to succeed, despite the odds.

If you walk away with just one bit of advice from this book, it should be this: don't be afraid to change. Your change doesn't have to be dramatic. It might mean sacrificing something you love, but it is guaranteed to make a difference in your life. So turn the page and start feeling happier and more productive by casting off the fears and excuses that have been holding you back—until now.

1

FACE YOUR FEARS!

The Ten Most Common
Excuses for Not Changing

▶▶ ONE OF THE first things I ask my clients to do is to tell me why they think they haven't yet reached their goals. Inevitably, the same excuses come up again and again. These justifications for failure are sometimes well founded, sometimes imagined, but in either case, people use them to confirm their preexisting belief that their lives can't get better. It gives them a reason to be discouraged—and *not* to try.

People resist change because they are afraid of the unknown. Only when a situation becomes too painful are people motivated to make a change. Don't wait for your life to become unbearable. Begin your transformation process now! It's easier and less daunting if you make one small change at a time, rather than attempting a total overhaul down the road. If you use any of the excuses described in this chapter, you can free yourself from those shackles of defeat by applying my simple three-part strategy: change one thing, dump one thing, and keep one thing. Let's begin by looking at the ten most common excuses.

Excuse 1: I'm Not Educated

Whenever people tell me they are not educated, I ask what they mean by this. Does "not educated" mean you don't have a high school or college degree, or that you don't have the right training in your desired field? Not being educated doesn't mean you aren't smart. You can have street smarts, which can certainly help you in business, or you can be bright but not book smart. And while I encourage people to get some kind of degree in order to compete in this increasingly tough marketplace, college isn't for everyone. Keep in mind that many highly successful people, including Bill Gates, Steve Jobs, Harry Truman, Walt Disney, Peter Jennings, Abe Lincoln, and George Washington, did not graduate from college, so you're in good company.

Generally, when people believe they were passed over for a job or promotion because they lack a college degree, they do one of two things. The first is they tend to overcompensate by being aggressive. The second is they keep an extremely low profile so no one notices their knowledge gap. Aggressive people have a tendency to intimidate others. They have trouble letting things go. And if one of their ideas isn't well received, they assume it's because people don't respect their expertise. The low-profile person will try to stay under the radar by not volunteering for projects or not speaking up in a meeting or other group setting.

Change one thing: If one of these scenarios describes you, you need to change the way you communicate. To do that, you should videotape yourself in action. It can be in a business setting, while you are at a party, or when you're on vacation. It doesn't matter, as long as you are interacting in a group situation. If you don't have a video of yourself, ask someone you trust to interview you on camera.

When I do this with clients, I start by asking softball questions and follow up with something that will make the interviewee angry or uncomfortable. It's important to do this so the client can see how he or she reacts when the going gets tough. Here are some sample questions I use:

▶ Tell me a little about yourself.
▶ Tell me about your job or work life.
▶ What's the best thing that has happened to you this year?
▶ What's the biggest challenge you've ever faced?
▶ What makes you angry?

The interview should last about thirty minutes or until you get a full range of emotions. Afterward, sit down with the interviewer and as many people as you can think of whom you trust to be candid, and have them comment on what they see. Have them pay attention to your body language, your facial expressions, and the kinds of words you use. Do you seem friendly and approachable? Are you defensive? Do you slouch or sit with your arms folded?

When I started giving workshops, people used to tell me that I was intimidating. I thought they had to be mistaken. Me, intimidating? But when I watched myself on tape, I couldn't believe how scary I was! After another presentation, someone told me that I didn't smile enough; I looked too grim. Again, I didn't realize I was coming across as so serious and unapproachable until I saw a tape of myself speaking. Since then, I've made a concerted effort to smile more whenever I speak in public.

If you are not sure whether you are someone who likes to stay under the radar, ask yourself these questions: Do people make eye contact with you when you are in a meeting, or do they look right past you? If coworkers are gathering a group together to go out to lunch, are you left out? If you feel like you are invisible, it's time for you to speak up. When you go to meetings, take a cheat sheet on which you've listed talking points that you want to discuss before it's over. At the very least, say, "I agree with that," when someone makes a good point or, "I'm not sure about that," if you disagree. Make sure you are heard. Practice as much as possible in a comfortable setting, such as the next time you go out with friends or family.

Dump one thing: Drop the idea that you need to get a degree in order to be successful. If you can't get the degree you want, you should join an organization where you can surround yourself with educated people. Learn from them. The degree doesn't matter as much as being up-to-date with the latest developments in your field or profession. Start with taking a course, getting a certification in your field, or joining a professional association. Once you are sure that you want to make the commitment, you can look into applying to a college or university and use some of the connections you made as references.

Gail, 46, worked for a Fortune 500 company but did not have a business degree even though she had been in the financial services industry for years. Because of this, she felt as though her team did not respect her. Family obligations prevented Gail from going back to school, so I advised her to get a certification in one of the financial software programs used at her company. Getting that certification gave her the confidence she needed. Gail is now her company's director of finance.

You can also read books and listen to educational tapes while you are in your car, at the gym, or doing errands. All these efforts will help you build a foundation of knowledge and boost your confidence.

Keep one thing: Establish what it is you bring to the party, and give yourself some credit. Maybe you are a good mediator or someone who is able to spot typos and other mistakes. Your accomplishments don't have to be huge. To keep yourself motivated, make a list of your strengths, and read it every day before you go to work and before you go to bed. I also recommend finding a successful "business guru" and using his or her guidelines every day to keep you motivated. Stephen Covey, author of *The 7 Habits of Highly Effective People*, was my guru when I began my consulting practice. His advice kept me going for years and still does.

Excuse 2: I Don't Speak So Good

As a child of immigrants, I understand the problems people face when English is not their first language. People sometimes think you are stupid if you stumble over a word, use one incorrectly, or miss a cultural reference. But people from other countries aren't the only ones who don't speak well. I've encountered people who mumble, speak too fast (something I had to work on), speak too slowly, or use inappropriate language. Having the proper communication skills is one of the most important gateways to success in both your professional and your personal life. (See Chapter 6 for advice on changing your communication style.)

Change one thing: Practice your enunciation by reading a paragraph with a pencil in your mouth. Then take the pencil out of your mouth and read the paragraph two more times. Do this exercise every day for a month. It really works for diction and pronunciation because it teaches you to use more of the muscles in your mouth. Record yourself so you can hear the difference.

When Aashan, a 33-year-old actuary from Illinois, came to me, his accent was so heavy that his coworkers couldn't understand what he was saying. People would ask him to repeat himself or would just give up altogether. After Aashan did the pencil exercise for thirty days, his enunciation and speaking pace improved tremendously. When he made his next presentation, it was so well received that his colleagues described him as being the star of his office. Aashan also improved his presentation by choosing words that were easy to pronounce and staying away from difficult words.

Keep one thing: Having an accent can be part of your personality, so unless you are going into broadcasting, you don't need to erase it entirely. If you think your accent is holding you back, ask your friends to tell you whenever you mispronounce a word. It can be embarrassing at times, but eventually you will learn by listening to the way the words should be spoken.

Dump one thing: Don't try to pronounce difficult words. It's not necessary to use a big word when a smaller one will suffice. It's better to be understood than to impress people with your vocabulary.

Here are some other things you can do:

▶ **Watch TV.** If you are just learning English, watching TV can be an entertaining way to learn colloquial speech. Use the closed-caption mode on your TV so you can read any phrases that you missed or didn't understand.

▶ **Record yourself.** Get a tape recorder or other recording device and listen to yourself reading passages from a book. If you don't have a tape recorder, call your cell phone or answering machine, leave messages, and listen to yourself that way.

▶ **Listen to audiobooks.** Spoken-word CDs and podcasts are an excellent way to learn a language or improve your English skills. Download a podcast to your MP3 player, or get CD recordings from your bookstore or library, and then listen while you are commuting.

▶ ANNA'S REALITY CHECK ▶▶▶

Sometimes we just have to face our fears and go for it! You might not be able to speak as well as Barack Obama, but there are ways to make presentations easier:

▶ Keep it short. Why prolong the pain for either you or the audience?

▶ Use handouts. Give people something to look at and read along with; it takes some of the pressure and eyes off of you. We might think presentations are all about us, but they're not. They are about content and sharing information.

▶ Ask questions. A presentation is always more interesting when you get the audience involved. Plus, the more the audience speaks, the less you have to.

Continued

> ▶ Find friendly faces in the audience. People usually smile when you make eye contact with them, so search the room for smiling faces that will make you feel more comfortable while talking.
> ▶ Have a strong opening and closing. The opening sets the tone for your presentation, and the closing wraps up what you've said, whether your presentation is for the purpose of informing or for selling an idea. These are the most important parts of your presentation—and will be the most memorable if you do them well.

If you are having trouble fixing your language problems or until you get better, select a job where you don't have to speak much. I know a smart, attractive man who stuttered whenever he was asked to speak publicly. He wanted to go into advertising, so he studied to be an art designer, where he worked with computer images and rarely had to go to meetings or give presentations. He eventually became an art director at a major New York firm. In his case, a picture was worth a thousand words *and* thousands of dollars!

Excuse 3: I Don't Have Enough Experience

Lack of experience is one of the most common excuses I hear, but fortunately, it is also the most easily fixed. Susan, a 35-year-old woman from Minneapolis, told me she wanted to go into accounting. She had an associate's degree in business but had never done accounting professionally. She gave up the idea of trying because she felt it was hopeless, given her lack of experience. Instead of giving up, I advised her to volunteer to do the books for a nonprofit organization. She ended up working for a local charity that couldn't afford to hire someone. It was a great job to add to her résumé, and it eventually led to her getting a high-paying accounting position.

Change one thing: Volunteer for an organization that will give you the experience you need, the way Susan did. Don't take on too big a project at first. Instead of going to the United Way, for example, try a small group that needs your help such as the local animal shelter or day care center. There's going to be a learning curve, so you will need some time to work your way up. If you want to be an interior decorator, start by offering to redo at least three of your friends' houses. I started my business by working with friends first.

Keep one thing: Keep a record of your successful projects. Take before-and-after pictures, if appropriate, or gather testimonials to put on a website advertising your services. (Yes, you should build a professional website—it's worth the investment, which need not be large.) You can follow up by joining associations in your industry and getting the proper accreditation.

Dump one thing: Don't be afraid to try something new just because you haven't done it before.

Excuse 4: I'm Too Smart

Nobody wants to work with someone who thinks he or she is smarter than everyone else. While know-it-alls often succeed in spite of themselves, they alienate others with their condescending attitude and usually end up working on their own rather than on a team. These people are the opposite of those who stay under the radar. They are braggarts who think most jobs are beneath them.

One of my clients is a successful financial institution in Chicago. One day, the person who opened up the bank each morning was sick, and no one could get into the building. Someone called the corporate office, and the CEO of the company happened to pick up the phone. When he learned that everyone was locked out, he got the keys and opened the bank himself. Sure, he could have asked someone else to do this simple task, but he didn't. A good leader doesn't think he or she is above doing any job.

I work with many young people right out of college who are unwilling to take a low-level job. This is especially true of those who graduated from Ivy League schools. They want to go straight to the top or to the middle without paying their dues. I tell them if they hold out for a certain salary or position for too long, it might not happen. Internships are a great way to learn on-the-job skills from the bottom up, and there is nothing demeaning about being an apprentice.

Change one thing: Listen before you speak. Know-it-alls tend to be impatient and interrupt others. They believe their way is the only way. Ask questions instead of immediately coming up with all the answers. Instead of putting other people's ideas down by saying, "We've done this already," or "That will never work," take a gentler approach by saying, "Have you tried doing it this way?"

Keep one thing: Hang on to your self-confidence. Influence others by example, not by giving orders. In an ideal professional situation, all people should feel they are smart enough and have the right stuff to handle any situation.

Dump one thing: Stop taking credit for everything. Make sure you give credit to others for coming up with good ideas. If you're the boss, you will get the credit in the long run. It's better to be seen as a team player than as a lone wolf.

Excuse 5: I'm Unattractive

Studies have shown that attractive people tend to be more successful and make more money than those who are not blessed with beauty. It's not fair, but it's a fact. That said, you should not give up just because you don't look like Angelina Jolie or Brad Pitt. The first question I ask people who feel unattractive is what they would like to change about their appearance. Once we determine what that is, we can start working on ways to improve or camouflage our weaknesses. So much help is available to us today in terms of clothing and cosmetics that there is no reason to throw yourself a pity party.

The next thing I ask people who feel unattractive is what they *like* about themselves. This question is usually more difficult than the first one, but most people can find at least one thing they like, whether it's their eyes, hair, smile, or sense of humor. Whatever it is, you can build on your strengths and make sure you emphasize your positive features.

If you are overweight, ill-fitting clothes will make you look worse. Whether you are a tall man or woman, a jacket that falls in just the right place can make all the difference. If you're a short woman, buy a fashionable skirt that shows more leg, or add a few inches to your heels. There are shops and websites that cater to the plus-sized and petite woman. If you don't go to a specialty shop, go to a tailor. Men already know about the importance of owning a tailored suit. It's worth the extra money to have clothing that fits your size and figure, whatever it may be. (See Chapter 2 for more ideas about wardrobe and Chapter 3 for improving your body image.)

Change one thing: Nearly every woman can benefit from a little makeup—not the Kabuki kind, but the natural-looking, face-enhancing kind. If I had to choose only one perk-me-up cosmetic, it would have to be lipstick. Go to a professional who isn't selling a particular product to help you find the right shade for your age and complexion. Follow up with a good hairstyle, which is one of the most important changes you can make. When you visit the hair stylist, take him or her some pictures from magazines of hairstyles that you would like. Make sure, however, that the model's face shape and hair texture are similar to your own; otherwise, the style won't work. If you're over 40, look for inspiration in an age-appropriate magazine such as *More*.

Nowadays, there are more cosmetic products available for men than ever before, including moisturizers such as Clinique for Men, Clarins for Men, and Anthony Logistics, as well as shampoos and conditioners by Crew, Woody, and Matrix for Men, so there is no excuse for guys not to spruce up. I also recommend getting a Conair nose- and ear-hair trimmer for good facial grooming and a self-bronzer such as Angel by Thierry Mugler if you are pale. *Men's Health, Men's Journal,* and *GQ* magazines all provide great tips on fashion and grooming for the sophisticated man.

Keep one thing: Go to your closet, and find the one item you feel good in. When you find items that make you feel good about yourself, buy them in different colors so you can wear your favorite confidence-building clothing often.

Dump one thing: While you're in your closet, get rid of clothing that doesn't work for you. You might be crazy about a pair of pants that is just not flattering to you, so you need a second opinion. If you can't afford an image consultant like me to come in and purge your closet, get a friend to tell you what looks good and what doesn't. If an item of clothing gets the thumbs down, dump it and don't look back!

Excuse 6: I Was Fired from My Last Job

As traumatizing as getting fired or laid off can be, it no longer carries the kind of stigma it once did. With the economy the way it is, many people are now facing cutbacks or have been laid off at least once in their career. What do you do if you were fired for cause? Own up to why you were let go. Acknowledge what you did wrong, and come up with solutions so it won't happen again. If you didn't have the necessary skills, get them. If you refuse to admit that you might have done something to cause the firing, you risk repeating your mistake in your next job.

I recall one client who was fired because she didn't have computer skills. Her job required her to know Word, Excel, and PowerPoint, but all she knew how to do was turn the computer on. She tried to teach herself these programs, but her employer complained that she wasn't learning them fast enough, and she was let go. Although she was upset and frightened that she would have trouble getting another job, I advised her to take the necessary time to get the proper computer skills before she started her search.

I truly believe that being fired can be an opportunity to get an even better job. If you don't like the area you were working in, move to another one. And if your industry is changing, you need to learn additional skills so you can make a transition to a job that is more in demand. You might have to dip into your savings or take an interim job just to pay the bills, but it'll be worthwhile in the long run.

Change one thing: Don't play the victim. Remember that business is business, and don't take being let go personally. Always leave with grace and with your head held high. Next, you must put a good spin on what happened. If the job is on your résumé, interviewers will ask why you left. You can explain a personality conflict by simply saying, "It wasn't a good fit."

Dump one thing: Never speak badly of your former employer, no matter how much you hated your job. Don't say, "It was a horrible place to work," or "My boss was insane," even if it was the seventh circle of hell. If your new employer calls to check references, negative statements will inevitably come back to bite you. Say instead, "My job was stressful at times, but it was a great learning experience."

Keep one thing: Stay optimistic and keep your spirits up. Getting fired or laid off is unpleasant, but it's not a death sentence. Remind yourself that a new and potentially better job is in your future.

Excuse 7: It's Too Late to Try Something New

The belief that it's too late for you to try something new is simply wrong, wrong, wrong! I believe it is never too late to learn something new. The problem with people who say this is that they are unwilling to network. Well, guess what? You have to explore in order to discover a new world. Whether you are adding to existing skills or learning new ones, you must be willing to network with other people in your field through professional organizations, trade magazines, blogs, and websites, so you can stay on top of the latest trends.

Change one thing: If you have trouble networking, partner with someone in your field, and do it together. Not only is it more fun to network with someone else, that person can do some of the networking for you and help build your confidence whenever it flags. Think of it as the opportunity to add to your circle of business associates. You've heard the old saying: "It's not *what* you know, it's *who* you know."

Dump one thing: Lose the idea that you have to go to four networking events a week. Rather than being all over the place, pick and choose the right events to attend. It's more important to network efficiently than to do it often. Once or twice a week is plenty.

Keep one thing: Try to hold on to your enthusiasm for what you are doing. If the job has gotten stale, add a new challenge that will keep you motivated, or learn a new skill so you can transition into something you like better.

Excuse 8: I'm Too Old

If you're holding back because you say you're too old, the first question you must ask yourself is this: Do you *feel* like you are too old, or do you *look* like you are too old? There's a big difference. Most people, when asked, feel at least ten years younger than their chronological age. There are people who are 35 and look like they are 50, and those who are 50 and look 35. It's all a matter of perception and taking good care of yourself, both mentally and physically. Changing the way you think about yourself is the first and easiest way to knock years off the calendar.

Of course, you must also pay more attention to your face and body as you age. It is essential that you exercise in order to increase your metabolism, flexibility, muscle mass, and bone strength as you get older. There are also myriad skin products and makeup that can help you look your best. Your choice of what to use depends on your individual features, complexion, and budget. To get personal advice, go to a professional makeup artist. (For more ideas, see Chapter 3 on body image and Chapter 7 on self-image.)

In addition to maintaining a youthful attitude and appearance, you must stay plugged in. Tune into MTV or VH1 from time to time, and read an entertainment magazine so you are aware of the latest trends in music and pop culture. Talk to younger people about what's going on in their world.

Change one thing for women: The most important change a woman of a certain age can make is to her hair. It's OK to go gray if and only if you have a fabulous hairstyle. For this, you should go to a professional stylist to see what's right for you. In most cases, however, it is best to get rid of the gray. Don't be afraid to change your hairstyle. You don't have to go short the minute you turn 40, but you do need a flattering style that won't emphasize what gravity has driven south.

Kathy, a social worker from Long Island in her late 30s, came to me after her husband had left her for a younger woman. She was recently divorced and depressed about her situation, which was reflected in the way she looked. She had gray hair, didn't bother with makeup, and wore shapeless clothes that did not accentuate her figure. She wanted to do something to feel better about herself.

The first thing I had her do was take a personality test and color analysis to see how far we could take her out of her comfort zone. We got rid of the gray and added a golden brown color to her hair with high- and lowlights that lit up her face. Then we changed her bob to a more free-flowing style. Next we used Bobbi Brown makeup to add more color to her cheeks and lips.

▶ ANNA'S REALITY CHECK ▶▶▶

Never wear clothes that skew too young in an attempt to look youthful. Women, stay away from low-rise jeans, thongs, baby doll dresses and miniskirts. If you can pinch an inch around your middle, get a pair of body shapers such as Spanx or Donna Karan Intimates. Shapewear will create a smooth silhouette while making you look five pounds thinner. Men, don't get any tattoos or body piercings, no matter how trendy or chic they seem at the time. That flag you have inked on your chest when you are 20 will be flying at half mast by the time you reach middle age and beyond!

I also changed the color of her clothes from dull, mousy browns to warmer browns, whites, and off-whites and crisp shirts in lively colors. Then we updated her shoes and handbags. With her new look, Kathy felt much better about herself and was able to move to a younger community, where she joined social groups and started dating.

Change one thing for men: Invest in at least one expensive, tailored suit. This is a good foundation upon which you can build by adding a dress watch, a good pair of dress shoes, a blazer, and a black wool dress coat. If only it were so easy to complete a woman's wardrobe!

Dump one thing for women: Stay out of the sun. Dermatologists have been warning about this for decades; I can't understand why more people don't heed their message. One of the reasons a baby's skin is so soft is that it has yet to be ravaged by the sun. A tan may look healthy, but sun damage causes wrinkles and possibly skin cancer. If your skin is pale and you need more color, a bronzer or self-tanner will pick up the slack.

Dump one thing for men: Never, ever do the comb-over or wear a toupee! There's no shame in being bald, and there are many examples of actors and athletes who wear their shiny domes with pride. For men, salt-and-pepper hair works best, so ask your stylist about rinses that only partially remove the gray.

Keep one thing: Keep your sense of humor. Why is it that so many of us get crabbier as we get older? Yes, the more years we live, the more we understand that life is hard, but try not to take yourself and the world around you too seriously. Humor can be a coping mechanism when times are tough, and not only has it been proven to make us feel better, it also helps us move up in business.

According to an article in the *New York Times*, a study of 737 chief executives of major corporations found that 98 percent would hire an applicant with a good sense of humor over one who seemed to lack one. Another study, reported in *Harvard Business Review*, found that coworkers who were described by executives as having a sense of humor moved up the corporate ladder more quickly and earned more money than their peers.

Excuse 9: The World Is Against Me

People who blame their inability to succeed on others can be dangerous in the workplace. Rich, a 38-year-old information technology manager who came to me from Dallas, used to pit one coworker against another. He would twist around what people said to him so it sounded negative. No one trusted him, and his colleagues did their best to avoid working with him.

He actually did this with me during one of our sessions. I asked him what his biggest challenge was, and he told me his boss was preventing him from getting the promotion that he felt qualified for. I told him he had to start by selling himself to others around him, so he could summon the support to get his boss to change his mind. The following week, I got a call from Rich's boss, who asked me why I had told Rich that he shouldn't trust him anymore. Of course, that's not at all what I had said. I was furious!

The reason Rich said this was that he thought everyone, including me, was against him. He believed that the world wanted him to fail. His brand of one-upmanship helped make him look better by bringing other people down. It took a long time, but we eventually fixed his problem by convincing him that people actually wanted to help, not hurt him.

I asked Rich to videotape himself at work and then watch the tape with the sound off to see if his body language was sending signals that he was angry. He saw how he rarely made eye contact, frowned all the time, and sat with his arms folded in a defensive posture. It took a number of sessions, but by practicing in front of the mirror, he eventually learned how to smile more often. The change was so enormous that his daughter asked him why he was so cheerful!

Change one thing: Turn adversaries into allies. Get to know your coworkers in a social setting by taking them out to lunch or for a drink after work. Try to enlist the people you think are against you as allies by getting to know them as people rather than as competitors. Socializing outside the office will allow you to relax and show a bit of your softer side. If you are uncomfortable with what someone has said to you, ask for clarification rather than jump to conclusions, and try not to take constructive criticism personally.

Dump one thing: Get rid of the notion that you are in it alone. You must understand the importance of working as a team. If you are having trouble communicating with others calmly in the workplace, find someone who can be your spokesperson and make a case for you at meetings.

Keep one thing: Keep your burning desire to succeed and to stay on top of your game, but try to chill out.

Excuse 10: No One Takes Me Seriously

Unlike those who think everyone is against them, people who think no one takes them seriously are generally well liked. The reasons they are often not taken seriously by their colleagues are that they joke around, use inappropriate language, dress in a quirky fashion, or are habitually late.

Sandy, a managerial trainer who worked at a fast-food restaurant in Atlanta, had a reputation as being fun but glib. She worked with people who were not well educated, so she thought joking around was a way to connect with them. Although she was well liked, she was not able to shift styles when working with senior management, who expected her to behave more professionally.

If she was late to work, she would say, "Well, you know how it is—I got hit by a car and had to go to the hospital, and the ambulance took 15 minutes to show up." Not only was this not funny, she was being dismissive about her tardiness. She thought she could minimize the situation by making a joke.

Change one thing: Think before you speak. Pause between sentences to give yourself time to assess the situation and select the appropriate thing to say. It might take a while to change, but remember that the first thought that comes into your head might not be the best one. Pay attention to your tone. If you speak with a little-girl voice, you will be thought of as a little girl. If you talk too loud, you might come off as abrasive. Record your voice, and ask someone who doesn't know you to describe what type of person they think you are just by listening to the way you speak.

Dump one thing: Stop fidgeting. People who flip their hair, tap their toes or fingers, or snap gum are difficult to take seriously—

or even be in the same room with! See my tips on changing your bad work habits in Chapter 4, which will help you get rid of potentially self-sabotaging ticks.

Keep one thing: Keep your personality, which can be winning. As I mentioned earlier, humor can be a bonding force in the workplace and helps make a difficult task much more fun. It's great to be well liked, but you must also be well respected.

2

THE CLOTHES MAKE
THE MANAGER

Change One Thing About
Your Wardrobe

▶▶ LET ME START with the good news. You don't need to go on a diet or get Botox to look younger, thinner, or cuter. This can be accomplished simply by giving your old, tired wardrobe a makeover. Likewise, if you are fresh out of college and want to add some gravitas to your image résumé, this can also be done with well-made, well-fitting clothes. In today's competitive business climate, it is more important than ever to exude confidence, so you earn the respect of your colleagues, clients, and the public. And nothing makes you feel more self-assured than looking fabulous.

According to a 2008 survey of more than 2,500 employers by CareerBuilder.com, 41 percent said that people who dress better or more professionally are promoted more often than those who do not. More than half of the employers in the financial industry said this is the case. It's *that* important. This chapter is about how to choose the right fit, fabric, and color the next time you go clothes shopping, so you will put your best well-heeled foot forward.

Unfortunately, without a one-on-one consultation, I can't tell you what you need to change about your wardrobe in order to achieve the image you want. The type of clothing you should wear depends on your size, complexion, and hair color. That said, the following self-assessment test will help you determine for yourself what you need to change about your style. Wearing the right skirt or jacket, for example, can hide a multitude of flaws, and I will tell you what's best for your particular needs. My image makeover tips include some general rules and advice that I have taught my clients and students over the years, along with simple guidelines for accentuating your positive features and avoiding the most common style mistakes.

As always, start by changing your biggest problem area first, and then work your way down the list, so you don't get overwhelmed by the transformation process. Even a small change can make a big difference, and the positive feedback you get will motivate you to continue. Keep in mind, this isn't about being the most fashionable person in the room; it's about looking polished and professional!

▶▶ ANSWER TRUE OR FALSE:

1. I look my best 90 percent of the time.
2. I have no trouble deciding what to wear each morning.
3. I have the right outfit to wear for an interview or presentation.

4. I know what fabrics look best on me.
5. My clothes send the appropriate message to my peers.
6. I dress appropriately for my industry.
7. My eyewear is less than three years old.
8. My shoes, belts, and briefcases are in excellent condition.
9. I have a travel wardrobe.
10. I have at least one suit that is less than three years old.
11. I update my entire wardrobe once a year.
12. All the items in my closet are in top condition.
13. I have appropriate clothing to wear to a formal or black-tie event.
14. I have appropriate clothing to wear to a company-sponsored sporting event.

Answers:

Please keep in mind that the following answers and explanations are designed to help you make the best decision for your individual situation. Everyone is different, so you should always use your judgment about what works for you based on your particular circumstances and personality.

1. *True.* It is impossible to look good 100 percent of the time, so if you make the effort to look your best most of the time, you are already ahead of the game. If this statement is true for you, then your clothes show the world that you are in charge of either your profession or your life. Clothing should enhance your feelings of confidence by making you look and feel great.

2. *True.* The more organized your closet is, the less trouble you will have deciding what to wear each day. You should organize your wardrobe by putting your tops, sweaters, jackets, and slacks together. Everything in your closet must fit you properly and be no more than three years old. (The exception to this rule is keeping a few trendy items that are in excellent condition and that you absolutely adore, which might come back into style down the road.) Your closet should also contain clothes for evening, casual, and formal wear. If you wear ensembles, by which I mean a top that goes with a skirt or pants, organize your closet by ensemble sets, so you don't have go on a search party to find your outfit each morning.

3. *True*. When you are going on an interview or giving a presentation, it is especially important to wear the most powerful-looking outfit in your closet, so you look and feel confident. All eyes are on you, and your interviewer or audience is sizing you up based, at least initially, on how you are dressed. If you don't yet own an "interview suit," go out and get yourself one. Every businessperson should own at least one great-looking suit.

4. *True*. Health-conscious people read the label for ingredients they will be putting in their body, and style-conscious people should be equally aware of what they are putting *on* their bodies. Fabric is about how a garment feels and fits. Clothing made of unnatural fabrics like polyester, rayon, and acrylic blends will make you feel warmer in the summer and colder in the winter. They do not mold well to the body. Natural fabrics like wool or cotton are more comfortable and breathable. If you are allergic to wool and find that it makes you itch, stick to cotton.

5. *True*. How do you want your friends to see you? You can express more about your personality with your casual wear, so think about what message you want to send. If you always wear frumpy clothes in public when you aren't at work, your peers will probably think you're a frump.

6. *True.* You should always dress appropriately for your particular business and stay in line with the company dress code, if there is one. Jeans and T-shirts might be acceptable in creative fields like publishing, advertising, or high-tech, but they are not right for the financial industry. Casual Friday does not mean shorts and flip-flops. On casual days, men should wear chinos and make sure their shirt has sleeves and buttons.

7. *True.* Nowadays, eyewear has become as much of a style statement as clothes, which is why many designers have a line of glasses and sunglasses. If you have been wearing the same old specs for years now, it's time for an upgrade. Choose the right style for your face shape, age, and profession.

8. *True.* A great way to update your style is by buying elegant accessories. Make sure your shoes, belts, and briefcases are well made, all leather (sorry, vegetarians), and in good condition. The only exception to the three-year rule is the briefcase; a well-worn high-end briefcase will have more of a presence than a well-maintained cheap one.

9. *True.* Having a wardrobe that you can take on the road is essential for the stylish businessman or -woman. Make sure that the clothes you take are easy to pack and maintain. Your suitcase shouldn't have clothes in more than three colors, and they should be made of fabrics that resist wrinkles. You will probably need two pairs of shoes, one for walking around and another for meetings. If you travel frequently, buy two of all your toiletries—one for your bathroom and one for your travel case. This way you are less likely to forget to pack something you need, which happens when you try to transfer items from your bathroom to your suitcase.

10. *True.* It is in the best interests of the retail and fashion industry to change styles almost every year in order to keep people buying. This makes it difficult to wear the same suit for more than three years and not look dated. Men have it easier than women when it comes to updating, because the biggest changes in men's suit styles tend to be the shoulders and jacket cut. When it comes to slacks, it's usually pleats or no pleats.

11. *False.* You don't have to give your wardrobe a complete overhaul every year, but you can update it by getting one or two new items that you can add to your old faithfuls.

12. *True.* If you answered False to this question, then you must go through your closet and throw out or donate anything that is worn, torn, faded, stretched, and out of style. Wearing any such clothes will give the impression that you don't respect yourself.

13. *True.* Even if you're not a head of state, chances are you will be invited to at least one wedding that is formal or black tie. For these occasions, men should own a top-of-the-line tuxedo shirt, tie, and cummerbund. You can rent the tux if you don't want to own one. For formal events that are black tie optional, you can pull out your power suit. For women, a black evening dress never goes out of style, so buy one if you know you will be going to at least one formal event within the year. Women who do not want to wear a dress or skirt because they don't like the way their legs look can opt for palazzo (flared) pants instead.

14. *True.* One of the most common mistakes people make is thinking that weekend wear is acceptable for a corporate sporting event, which is when senior management or clients go to a company-sponsored event. In these cases, it is fine to dress casually, but never wear cut-offs, halter tops, or flip-flops. Like casual Fridays, corporate events call for modified business casual. Shorts (preferably the cargo style for men) with docksiders or loafers (with no socks) in the summer and a new sweatshirt in winter are acceptable. Never wear socks with sandals, no matter how comfortable you think that is! It's better to suffer than look like a dork.

Wear Your Clothes, Don't Let Your Clothes Wear You

Like makeup and hairstyles, clothes create a visual impression that should be natural, not fake or flamboyant. You would be surprised how many people I see who think they are expressing their personality by wearing outfits that are gaudy or ill fitting (too big or too small for their frame). This is what I mean when I say you shouldn't let your clothes wear you. Unless you are in show business and it is part of your job to stand out, you shouldn't wear sequins, large flowery patterns, or fringe, especially to work. Likewise, clothes that are the wrong color for your complexion, are decades out of style, or are made of a fabric that wrinkles like a shar-pei can take on a life of their own. And over-accessorizing with jewelry, which includes men with flashy rings or gold chains, is not the way to express your individual style. The bottom line is that you don't want people to notice your clothing before they notice you. It is especially important to be in sync with your colleagues in the workplace, so never use the office as your personal runway.

Don't Buy Trendy Clothes Just Because They Are in Style Right Now

The fashion industry likes to create trends and trumpet them each year so you will always want to buy new clothes. Everyone is allowed one folly, so go ahead and buy one trendy item to add to your wardrobe each season. But unless it fits your face, color, body type, and personality, put it on the rack and not on your back. Black might always be in, but if it washes you out, find the color that works best for your complexion, and wear that.

Whatever you do, don't experiment with something new and trendy at work. Wear that high-impact outfit or hairstyle at a social event where the risk is low. If you were throwing a dinner party, would you make something you've never tested before or a tried-and-true dish that you know is a winner? The same goes for trying out new clothes and hairstyles.

▶ **CLOTHING STYLES: CLASSIC VERSUS TRENDY VERSUS FAD** ▶▶

- ▶ Classic styles have been around for more than seven seasons.
- ▶ Trendy styles typically last two to three seasons.
- ▶ Fads last one season.
- ▶ Sharp, current wardrobes blend classic and trendy clothing pieces.

Color Makes an Impact

What's the first thing you remember about what someone was wearing? If you are like me, it's the color. Color is like a song; you might not always recall the lyrics, but you will remember the melody. It makes a huge impact and can affect the way others view you. It is one of the first things clients ask me about during a consultation. Think seriously about your color choice if you want to make an impact and project a certain image, and make sure that color works for your complexion.

Studies have found that burgundy is considered a royal color with elitist overtones, and blue is conservative and traditional. The same goes for royal blue, which conveys a sense of tradition, responsibility, knowledge, and trustworthiness. It is the reason IBM adopted blue as its company color and had the "Big Blue" nickname trademarked in 1988, well after relaxing its dress code. There is no doubt that navy blue is one of the top choices for conservative business wear.

One client came to me because he had problems connecting to others and said people found him intimidating. He was built like a wrestler: large and stocky, with jet-black hair. To make matters worse, he wore a goatee and always dressed in black because, as he explained, he liked "earth tones." I explained to him that black is not an earth tone (brown and green are) and that his wearing all black made him look like a prince of darkness. I suggested he wear softer fabrics and lighter colors instead. Once he did, his entire persona seemed to change. If you want to be less intimidating, wear softer fabrics and softer colors like blue, brick, gold, or ecru (off-white).

Another of my clients had the opposite problem; he wanted to look more authoritative. When I met with him, he was wearing a yellow polo shirt, which made him seem approachable but made him look more like a car salesman than an executive. I

▶ WHAT YOUR FAVORITE COLOR SAYS ABOUT YOU ▶▶▶

Morton Walker's excellent book *The Power of Color* is about the psychological effects of color and how it is used in business to influence consumer behavior. According to Dr. Walker, when you favor one color over another, you are "telling a story about your personality and behavior." Interestingly, he says the person who hates all colors is also likely to hate music and children, and to be wary of the world in general. These psychological connections are further proof that color preference is not just an arbitrary choice, but also a little peek into your soul. Here's what Dr. Walker's book says about our colorful personality traits. Use it to reinforce your current image or to create a new one, but never wear a color that isn't right for your complexion just because it sends a certain message.

▶ Red. People who wear red tend to be outgoing, assertive, vigorous, moody, and impulsive. You sympathize with others and are easily swayed. You are also an optimist, but you do not hesitate to voice your opinions, even if they are complaints. Red is the most popular color with American consumers.

▶ Orange. Those who like orange are good-natured, sociable, and like red-lovers, easily swayed by other's opinions. They are good workers, have strong loyalties, and are kindhearted.

▶ Yellow. People who like yellow are imaginative, have a lot of nervous energy, are thoughtful, and have an interest in saving the world. They can also be aloof and more given to theory than to action. They are shy and secretly crave admiration and respect, but they make reliable friends and confidants.

▶ Green. If green is your favorite color, you are probably a good citizen who is aware of social customs and etiquette. Green people are candid and moral, make excellent teachers, and are extremely family oriented.

▶ Blue. Those who prefer blue are introspective, conservative, and likely to retreat to calmer waters during stressful situations. They are loyal friends who lead a simple, quiet life and keep a tight lid on their passions. They are intolerant of stupidity in others and of those who they think are smarter.

▶ Purple. If purple is your favorite color, you have a good mind and sharp wit, and you are a keen observer. You are vain, creative, quick to anger, and able to recognize greatness in others.

▶ Brown. It is no coincidence that "brown shirts" are people who perform their duties conscientiously. They are also shrewd and tight when it comes to money. They are steady Freddies who are dependable and not the least bit impulsive.

▶ Gray. Those whose favorite color is gray are cautious and seek calm and peace. They make good mediators because they are always trying to find a compromise that works for both parties.

▶ Black. People for whom black is their color of choice tend to be intelligent, worldly, conventional, proper, and polite. And while black can also mean you are prone to depression, you find it regal and dignified.

advised him to wear dark navy instead, which is a much more powerful color, and save the yellow polo for after hours.

As I said, you always need to keep your skin tone in mind when choosing a color. If you are African American or have a darker skin tone, you shouldn't wear black, because it will blend right in, but white or gray will create a beautiful contrast. If you have light skin, a pink shirt will give you a polished look.

Clothes Make a Statement About Power and Accessibility

Once you decide what kind of impression you would like to make, you can choose your clothes accordingly. If you are an executive businesswoman, the most powerful thing you can wear is a suit with a matching jacket and pants. In her bid to become the Democratic presidential nominee, Hillary Clinton wore the now-infamous pantsuit. While her color and style choices were sometimes questionable, and certainly not cutting edge in terms of fashion, it was the right choice for her, given that she wanted to project an aura of authority.

That said, unless you are planning to run for office or are a female executive who needs to exude power, the matching suit can appear too dated and matronly. Mismatched suits are much more contemporary, but make sure that the skirt or pants complement the jacket. A skirt that is tailored and straight lined is both authoritative and stylish, as is a straight-lined skirt that flares out at the bottom.

Conventional wisdom used to be that your boss is the best barometer for how to dress. The problem with dressing like your boss is that your direct superior might not be the best role model. One of my clients, who worked for an international Japanese corporation located in the United States, had a boss who was the nephew of the CEO. The boss wore his hair down to his shoulders, and his shirts were often unbuttoned and untucked. Even though he was my client's direct superior, he was obviously not the right person to use as a role model for how to dress. To

▶ ANNA'S DESIGNER SHOPPING LIST ▶▶▶

You certainly don't have to wear a designer label, but it won't hurt your image if you do. Your wardrobe should include at least one knockout item that makes you feel like you own the room. If you are not a dedicated follower of fashion, take this list along with you for guidance the next time you go shopping.

MEN

High end: Armani, Burberry, Hickey Freeman

Midrange: Joseph Abboud, Hugo Boss, Calvin Klein, Hart Schaffner Marx, Ralph Lauren, John Nordstrom, Jones New York, Alfani (Macy's label)

Tuxedos: John Varvatos Star, Armani, Joseph Abboud (Most of the men's designers make a tuxedo.)

WOMEN

High end: Armani, St. John, Hugo Boss, Dana Buchman, Landry

Midrange: Anne Klein, Eileen Fisher, DKNY, Tahari by ASL, Michael Kors, Jones, Ralph Lauren, Calvin Klein, O Oscar, Jones New York, AK

Petite: Michael Kors, JM Collections, Alfani, AK Petite

Plus sizes: Jones New York, JM Collections, Ralph Lauren, Charter Club (Macy's label), Eileen Fisher, Nordstrom's Caslon be safe, I tell my clients to look two levels above them for how to dress.

While it is still important to dress for the position you aspire to, the best rule of thumb is to wear something that makes you feel good and look good. It must also be appropriate to the workplace, so don't even think about going to work in that low-cut silk blouse that makes you look like a movie star.

Jewelry Should Be an Attraction, Not a Distraction

If worn correctly, accessories can be the jewel in the crown of your ensemble. Keep in mind, however, that when it comes to adorning your clothes or body, moderation is key.

▶ **Earrings for women.** Women should not wear chandelier earrings. They move around too much and are too distracting, especially if you give presentations or are going to be on camera. Wearing multiple earrings is OK if you are in a creative field where the dress code is more relaxed and you are free to express your personal style. It is not acceptable in finance, law, or medicine.

▶ **Rings and bracelets for women.** Do not wear more than two rings or bracelets if you are in a conservative business. Nowadays, single women are wearing rings on their middle finger. I am not a fan of this style, but it has become very popular with younger women. I see no reason why single women can't wear a ring on the ring finger of either hand, as long as it is not mistaken for a wedding ring. Many smart young women are wearing Yurman rings, which are a mixture of gold and silver.

▶ **Necklaces for women.** The stones on your necklace should never be larger than the length of your eye. This rule ensures that your jewelry will be in balance with the rest of your body. There are always exceptions, of course, but the buzzwords for jewelry are taste and balance. If you work for a conservative company, the classic pearl necklace is a safe choice, or you can wear a larger pearl bead if you want to look more contemporary. Also beware of pearls that are too tiny, because they can date you. If you are on the other side of fifty, you might want to get something a bit edgier, so you don't appear too stodgy. If you are petite, avoid wearing jewelry that is too large. Try wearing one large bead surrounded by smaller pieces.

▶ **Tattoos.** I realize that tattoos are now in the mainstream and are no longer the result of having had one too many; however, they still don't enhance a professional image in most cases. Here's the deal: If you are a corporate attorney who must have a tattoo, get it someplace where the sun don't shine. It can be your little secret.

▶ **Jewelry for men.** Gold chains, bracelets, and ornate wedding bands are not appropriate for men in the workplace. American men should stay away from wearing rings on the middle finger or pinkie at work (more widely accepted outside the United States); stick to the ring finger during office hours. Men who are in creative fields such as art, music, or film, however, can wear an earring.

▶ **Watches (men and women).** Stick with a good dress watch, as long as it's not ostentatious. Stay away from diamonds and other precious jewels in the workplace. Larger watches for women are now quite fashionable. Heavy style watches, especially the TAG, are very popular with men under 35.

The Three H's (Hair, Heels, and Hose)

Women ask me about the Three H's at nearly every seminar I give. It is a source of great confusion, made even more difficult by the depth-defying shoes and other fashions set by the hit TV show *Sex and the City*. Here's the scoop for today's stylish women.

▶ **Hair.** There is nothing more transforming than having a great hairstyle, so invest in yourself by going to a good stylist who will give you the right cut and color for your face and complexion. Both men and women should have hair that moves to avoid looking like an oversprayed TV anchor. I understand that Southern women (and Amy Winehouse) like big hair, but unless you are a country singer or in rehab, keep the skyscrapers off your head.

▶ **Heels.** Four-inch stilettos send a signal that you are a sexual person. Shoes that have extremely pointed toes are attractive but impractical for everyday use. Save them for after hours. The same goes for peep-toe shoes. I'm not fond of any open-toe shoe, because it draws attention to the fact that you're not wearing any hose.

▶ **Hose.** Every month, people from all over the world send me hundreds of e-mails with questions about pantyhose, so I know what a hot-button issue this is for many women. Almost all women say they hate wearing pantyhose, but most agree that if they have to give a presentation, attend an important meeting, or meet with a client, they must wear hose with closed-toe shoes. Wearing hose is especially important if you are an executive. This might change as corporate dress codes become less formal, but for now, you should invest in some pecan and off-black hose. No prints, no fishnets, no seams. And if you must go natural, invest in Dior or Calvin Klein, which are more expensive (around $10 a pair) but have a slight tint and last longer.

You *Can* Judge a Book by Its Cover

While women are always being judged on how they look, men who choose the right suits and shirts can make a favorable first impression as well, which is important in these highly competitive times. Like it or not, guys, people do form opinions about you based on how you look, including what you are wearing. Here are some tips for selecting a suit (and other assessories) that suits you best:

Suits

There's no question that the suit makes the man, and in the hierarchy of style, the good suit is king. A well-designed suit can make a man look successful, sophisticated, and chic. A pinstripe, a favorite of lawyers and investment bankers, can make a small man look tall or a chunky man look slim with soft wools. A good suit, like a loyal dog, is a man's best friend.

Every businessman worth his salt should invest in at least one good designer-brand suit that he can wear to see clients, go on interviews, or face the public. Eventually, you should have four suits, which can work for every season and occasion. If you, like many men, are unsure of what kind of suit suits you best, here are some general rules:

- ▶ The standard blue suit—by which I mean navy, not sky blue—is great for business lunches, politics, or casual parties. Select one with a slight weave, which will have a richer, more elegant look. It can be worn with black or brown shoes.
- ▶ The classic gray suit is appropriate for just about everything, and it looks good on most men, which makes it a safe choice. Grays can be patterned, but you can start with plain and work your way up to a slight stripe.
- ▶ The basic black is a perennial classic that never goes out of style. It is good for weddings, funerals (yours or someone else's), and even Mob parties, should you become a made man. Younger men seem to prefer black to navy, so I recommend a very dark navy that almost looks black.

Any of these suits can be worn with a pinstripe shirt. For summer, a lightweight olive, taupe, or camelhair is a good way to go.

No matter what style you choose, a suit needs to be fitted to your body. You've heard the expression, "she was hanging all over him like a bad suit." Your suit shouldn't look like you slept in it last night.

Clean your suit only once a season, because dry cleaning will wear out the fabric.

Trends in men's suits used to change every decade or so; now they have a shelf life of six months to a year. The fashion industry, which has been gasping for air of late, aims to keep you off your game, but there are general rules. Suits should be made of either wool or cotton. The exception is what I call the "warrior" suit for men who travel a lot, which can be a combination of polyester and wool fabric that won't wrinkle in a folded garment bag. If you want to make it a bit more interesting, you can buy a suit that has a weave or a minimal pattern that is either in the weave or in a slight color difference.

A suit jacket should be worn with suit pants, not with jeans or chinos. For more casual wear, buy a navy blazer or sport coat. If you buy a two-button jacket, you only need to button the top button. Ask me why, and I'll tell you, "Because I said so." Seriously, there is no other explanation except that not doing so will make you too stiff. For three-button suits, button either the middle button or the top two buttons. Once again, do not be tempted by the woefully ignored bottom button. Let it be.

With pants, the main questions are about whether you want pleats and cuffs. The question of whether or not your pants should have pleats depends on your body size. Men who have a little bit of a gut might be better off wearing a pleat. Those who are flat in front should not wear a pleat. Years ago, the prevailing wisdom was that cuffs should be worn only with pleated pants. Today, the fashion industry is challenging this idea. In general, cuffs give an old-school vibe. Decide based on what kind of image you would like to project. Whatever you choose, your pants should be crisp enough to be proudly worn without a jacket. If not, rethink and get thee to a tailor.

A belt of the right width will also keep your waistband from rolling over. If you're a full-figured man, choose pants with a dark lining in the waistband, so if it rolls over, you will not notice it. Put your wallet in the back pocket, and keep the front two pockets empty, or else risk someone quoting Mae West by asking if you are happy to see them.

If you are completely lost about what kind of suit to buy, I suggest you do what women do and look at a men's fashion magazine to get an idea of what's out there. A good starter suit would be dark navy or black. Barring that, men who are clueless about clothes should take a fashion-savvy friend along shopping or ask the salesperson, who *should* know his or her stuff. Nordstrom, Saks, and Neiman Marcus all have wonderful men's departments with very helpful staff.

Shirts

Back in the day, men always wore starched white shirts to work. Thankfully, there is now an array of colors and stripes available for dress shirts, with equally colorful ties to match. Take a look at *GQ* or *Details* to get an idea of how men's fashions have evolved over the years.

Sport shirts do not have a button-down collar, and they come in small, medium, or large. They should never be worn with a suit jacket and tie. If you want to dress them up a bit, wear a sport shirt with a blazer and khakis. If you hate to iron or send out your shirts, make sure the wrinkle-free shirts you buy have more cotton than synthetic fabric, to ensure that they will breathe.

French cuff shirts, which are the kind you wear with cuff links, are now being worn in New York without the jacket, but most men usually wear them with a jacket.

▶ **IS THE LOOK RIGHT FOR YOU? TAKE THE BLINK TEST** ▶▶▶

Stand five feet away from a mirror, close your eyes, and then quickly open them. If you like what you see, the outfit is a go. If you don't, it probably won't work. Your first impression is usually the right one.

Polo shirts are acceptable in creative businesses, but they are actually more difficult to maintain, because they must be laundered or else they get ruined. If you wear polos to work, you might have to take out your iron, and I'm not talking about the golf club.

The general rule for hosiery is to match your socks to your shoes: brown for brown, black for black. When in doubt, you are always safe with black. A light knit sock that isn't too bulky is your best bet for a business shoe. Never wear sport socks with dress shoes.

Something Expensive Will Look Cheap if It's Not the Right Fit

Good style has nothing to do with expensive clothes. A $50 shirt can look as good as a $250 dollar one if it has the right fit. Likewise, an ill-fitting garment, even one with a designer label, will look cheap. If you buy something off the rack that you think looks good on you and you have it professionally fitted, it will look expensive regardless of the price tag. The proviso is that the fabric must be good. Good fabric will mold to your body better.

> ▶ **PROPER FIT CREATES THE RIGHT LOOK** ▶▶▶
>
> ▶ To achieve a more expensive look, choose appropriate sleeve, hem, and jacket lengths.
> ▶ Avoid clothing that is too loose or too tight.

Don't Spend Too Much for Special Occasions and Too Little on Everyday Wear

I tell my clients that the biggest mistake people make is spending too much money on clothing for a special event like a wedding or graduation, and not enough on what they wear every day. Pull out the big bucks for clothes you wear to work every day, because you are going to live in them, and they need to look good. If you know that your clothes are going to get a lot of wear and tear, it's better to spend more so they will last.

▶ **REQUIREMENTS FOR YOUR CORE WARDROBE** ▶▶▶

Your core wardrobe should . . .

- ▶ Include a matched suit with a coordinating jacket and slacks
- ▶ Have clothing made of fabrics for three different seasons
- ▶ Contain either complete outfits or clothing that coordinates with three items already in your closet
- ▶ Have darker colors for a more powerful image
- ▶ Have high-contrast colors for a more dramatic look
- ▶ Have lighter colors for a more relaxed image
- ▶ Have neutral colors for a softer look
- ▶ Have shoes, belts, a briefcase, and purses made of leather
- ▶ Be the best quality you can afford

I did some modeling when I was younger, and the photo stylists would sometimes dress me in a well-fitted cheap outfit. They knew that the only thing I was going to do in it was stand still and pose, so the clothes didn't have to be expensive.

Style Means Never Having to Reinvent Yourself

Diana Vreeland, the former editor of *Vogue*, once said that style means never having to reinvent yourself. What she meant was that style is knowing what works for you, not for someone else. You shouldn't have to get up each morning and struggle with what to wear. Once you know what works for your age, coloring, and figure, you will know exactly what kind of clothes to buy.

Enhancing yourself is not the same as reinventing yourself. Sometimes you need to tweak or update your style a bit, but you never want to give up your integrity and your authenticity for the sake of fashion. Be true to who you are!

▶ A SUCCESSFUL IMAGE ▶▶▶

Your image is successful if it . . .

- ▶ Makes you feel attractive
- ▶ Makes you feel confident
- ▶ Is appropriate for the social or business settings in which you find yourself
- ▶ Is affordable in terms of purchase price and upkeep

Timing Is Everything

A fashion disaster from twenty years ago can be in fashion today. When I was a freshman in high school, my godmother gave me a puffy-sleeved blouse with yellow, orange, and red flowers on it. I wore it for a week with a red and yellow pleated wool skirt before a friend's mother told me that you should never wear flowers with pleats. Who knew that one day mix-and-match outfits would be in style? Timing is everything!

Do not give away vintage clothing that is well made, because it might come back in style. If the fabric becomes hard with time, however, you must give it up. Polyesters, even expensive ones, do not age well. But wools, silks, and blends have staying power. Designer Michael Kors says a good stylist knows how to edit, and someone who knows his or her style will know what to keep and what to toss.

MY BODY,
MYSELF

Change One Thing
About Your
Body Image

▶▶ WHEN PEOPLE ARE asked what they most want to change about themselves, nearly all have a criticism about the way they look. Even models can come up with something they dislike about their appearance. As the well-known affirmation says, you should change what you can and accept what you can't change— and try to make the best of it. Believe me, it can be done with the right clothing, makeup, hairstyle, and self-care.

The following self-assessment test will help you pinpoint the areas you should be working on.

▶▶ ANSWER TRUE OR FALSE:

1. I am happy with my body shape.
2. I sit straight in my chair.
3. I have good posture when standing.
4. My arms are relaxed against my body when I am listening.
5. My arms are relaxed against my body when I am speaking.
6. I exercise at least two or three times a week.
7. I brush twice a day and have regular dental checkups.
8. I update my fragrance every two years.
9. My nails are always clean and well groomed.
10. My feet are always well groomed.
11. I wash my hair at least every other day.
12. My hairstyle is less than three years old.
13. My height is just right.
14. I need to lose at least ten pounds.
15. I like the way I look in pictures.
16. I believe people when they compliment me on my physique.
17. I hate the way my nose looks.
18. I am always comparing my body to someone else's.
19. My clothes never fit right.
20. I never wear sleeveless shirts.
21. I can name three things I like about my body.
22. I like my face shape.
23. I like my skin tone.

Answers:

The following answers will help you decide what you need to change about yourself in order to have a better body image.

1. *True and False.* There is no right or wrong answer to this question, although it's better if you are happy with your body shape. Whatever the case, most of us do not have a perfect body, so we need to focus on the areas we like and find ways to camouflage our flaws.

2. *True.* Sitting up straight in a chair shows that you are confident and engaged with those around you. Slouching is not only sloppy and unattractive, it's disrespectful.

3. *True.* Bad posture is one of the most common problems I encounter as an image consultant. Did you know that you can look taller and thinner simply by standing up straight with your stomach in and your two feet firmly planted on the ground? I'm not saying you should look like a guard at Buckingham Palace, but imagine you have a string attached to the top of your head like a puppet and someone is pulling your head toward the ceiling. Did you feel how your spine just straightened out? There are even health benefits to standing up straight; for instance, if you suffer from back pain, chances are your posture needs correcting. Try standing against the wall to see how it feels to stand up straight, and make a conscious effort to correct your posture until it becomes second nature.

4. *True.* If you fold your arms while you are listening to someone speak, you will appear tense or defensive. Try to keep your arms in a comfortable, relaxed position when you are listening to someone speak. Putting your hands on your hips can make you look cocky, so put your hands in your pockets or intertwine your fingers in front of you if you feel as though you need to do something with them.

5. *True*. Your arms should also be as relaxed as possible when you are speaking. If you have a lectern, you can rest your hands on the top. When there's no lectern, you can hold a microphone or index card with notes while you walk around or use your hands to emphasize what you are saying. If your hands shake, don't hold a card, because it will flutter like a fan. Also, be careful not to gesticulate too much, or it will be distracting to your audience.

6. *True*. Exercising at least three times a week is essential to both your health and your psychological well-being. People spend thousands of dollars on products to help them lose weight and look younger, when exercising (combined with a healthful diet) can actually do both. Join a gym if you can afford to; get a fitness DVD if you can't. Aside from the cost of a good pair of athletic shoes, walking or running is free!

7. *True*. Your smile is one of the first things that people will notice about you, so it is essential that you brush at least twice a day and see a dentist once or twice a year. People are far more aware of their teeth today than ever before, which is why tooth whitening has become a billion-dollar industry. If your teeth are no longer pearly white, you can get them professionally whitened, have them laminated (most expensive), or use over-the-counter whitening strips to make your smile brighter. Be careful to not go too white or get caps that make your teeth look too big for your mouth.

8. *True*. Scents change with the times, so if you are still wearing Chanel No. 5, it's probably time for a change. The best fragrances are light, and outdoorsy scents are among my favorites. If you don't like or are allergic to fragrances, choose a bath or shower soap with a pleasant aroma. I like Neutrogena bath gel.

9. *True.* Manicures work for both women and men to get rid of cuticles, hangnails, and rough edges, so you don't scratch anyone when shaking hands. If you can't afford a professional manicure, go to a drugstore for a nail kit, and do it yourself.

10. *True.* Like fingernails, well-groomed feet are essential if you are wearing sandals or open-toe shoes. I find that pedicures, which come with a mini leg massage, are addictive! Once you get one, you're hooked. The well-dressed woman never shows her naked toes!

11. *True.* Whether you wash your hair every day or every other day depends on its texture, but one thing's for certain: greasy hair is not attractive. Wash yours however often is necessary to keep it looking clean and shiny. Generally, thick hair can be washed every other day, while thinner hair requires more attention.

12. *True.* If you are right out of college, you have probably worn the same hairstyle for four to six years. But once you enter the workforce, it's time for a style change so you don't scream "I'm an intern." If you are over 30 and have had the same style for three years or more, it's time to shake things up.

When your hair looks good, you will feel more confident. Period. This was confirmed by the Procter and Gamble–funded Yale Gender Communication Study, in which researchers asked 120 men and women to recall a bad-hair day. Participants recorded dips in self-esteem on those particular days. Surprisingly, men with bad-hair days are more likely than women to feel less confident about their performance. This is probably what keeps Rogaine in business.

13. *True.* Like body shape, height isn't something we can do much about, so we must find ways to enhance what we've got by choosing the right clothes—those that fit, however tall or small we are.

14. *True and False.* OK, so you may not be at your fighting weight right now; deal with it. Our weight is something that most of us can work on. Until you get to where you want to be, try to learn how to be comfortable with your weight right now. Again, having the right clothing and fit can make a molehill out of a mountain.

15. *True.* While some people are naturally photogenic, the majority of folks don't like the way they look in pictures. If you are comfortable mugging in front of the camera, you are probably on the right track as far as appearance is concerned!

16. *True.* The ability to accept compliments such as "You have a great figure" shows that you feel good about your physique. If you find yourself replying with some kind of dismissive statement ("You've got to be kidding—I have thunder thighs!"), then you've got some work to do, and I'm not talking about running on a treadmill.

17. *False.* We can't all have the profile of a Greek god, so short of rhinoplasty (a nose job), you should tell yourself that your less-than-perfect facial features give you character.

18. *False.* We are all born with different body types, so comparing your body to other people's is an exercise in frustration. Try to make the best of what you've got, and stop seeing how you stack up next to someone else.

19. *False.* If your clothes don't fit, you need to change your clothes, not necessarily your body, so read the section in this chapter on body shape to see what clothes fit your particular shape the best.

20. *True and False.* The answer to this question depends on the condition of your arms. Do they flap like the mops in a car wash because you have no muscle tone? If so, get yourself some free weights, and start working those triceps so you can feel better about exposing your arms. In the meantime, you should stay covered up by wearing long sleeves.

21. *True.* Whatever shape you're in, I urge you to find three things that you like about your body. If you're hippy, perhaps you are voluptuous on top. If your calves look more like bulls, you might also have beautiful shoulders. Men who are paunchy can have sexy, muscular legs. Make the most of the things you can boast of.

22. *True.* Your face is the star of the show, so if you think your face is too round, too oval, or you have a big chin like comedian Jay Leno, you will not be able to put your best face forward. I recommend going to a hair stylist for a cut that is just right for your face shape.

23. *True.* Skin tones vary based on your race, ethnicity, and, of course, genetics. If you have pale skin, there is plenty of makeup out there that will give you a healthy glow without your getting a decidedly unhealthy tan. Whatever your skin tone, take care of this vital organ by wearing sunblock every day.

Your Clothes Should Fit Your Body Type

One of the biggest mistakes people make is spending money on clothes that don't fit or flatter their shape. It will leave your pocketbook empty and your wardrobe looking weary. Making the right clothing choice for your particular figure not only will hide your flaws but also can highlight your best features.

A whopping 66 percent of the 63,000 people who responded to a 2008 AOL survey said they felt the least confident about their body shape compared with other parts of their body or face. The study underscores how important body image is to our self-confidence. The good news is that clothing can camouflage parts of our bodies that we don't like and highlight those areas we are most proud of. But before you pull out the credit card for some new clothes, you must first determine what kind of body shape you have.

To do this, start by looking at yourself naked in a full-length mirror. It's not always pleasant, especially if you're using a three-way mirror like the ones in the department stores, but it *has* to be done. Then decide which type of body you have, in terms of the following main body shapes:

▶ **Hourglass.** If your have broad shoulders, curvy hips, and a small waist, you are an hourglass. You probably have a small bone structure, medium-sized bust, and a bit of "back" or butt. This is one of the most sought-after shapes for women, because it is the most balanced and symmetrical. Hourglass women should not wear tight fabrics. Use thin or wide belts to highlight your smaller waist. Tunic tops that hug under the bust line and gently flare out look fabulous on this kind of figure. Streamlined pencil skirts or wide-waistband pants will hide a pouchy stomach, if you have one. Hourglass-shaped men should buy athletic-cut suits by Joseph Abboud, which favor broad shoulders and small waists. Pants with a pleated front will take care of the wide hips.

▶ **Inverted triangle.** You are an inverted triangle if you have broad shoulders, a full bust or chest, an average waist, narrow hips, and long legs. You are probably big boned and somewhat short-waisted. Women with this figure will want to deemphasize their upper half and emphasize their better half. You should stay away from frills and ruffles or busy patterned blouses, and avoid skirts or jackets that are too structured, heavy, or have shoulder pads. Fabrics made of silk, chiffon, or lightweight cottons work best for this kind of figure, as do pleated skirts and lower-rise jeans. Men who have this shape should avoid suits and jackets with wide lapels and those with and that are peaked, which accents the shoulders. Instead, choose softer, shoulder-style jackets and flap pockets that add balance to your body. Men with this kind of body type should buy sweaters with raglan sleeves (e.g., a sleeve that extends in one piece fully to the collar, leaving a diagonal seam from armpit to collarbone).

▶ **Apple.** Apple-shaped people have large busts or chests, wide backs, rounded midsections, and small bottoms. Because your upper body is wider than your lower half, apple-shaped women will want to minimize their large bust and thick waist and maximize their slim hips and gorgeous gams. Apple-shaped men can wear casual shirts under sweaters that are not tucked in at the waist and pants without pleats to create a seamless, smooth look.

Use a medium-width belt instead of one that is too thin or too thick.

Tight shirts will create a top-heavy look, so go with a flowing line such as a jersey knit, woven rayon, or nonclingy silks in drop-waist styles. The combination of a V-necked blouse and A-line skirt is especially good for a woman with this body type. If your arms are slender, show them off with sleeveless tunics and above-the-knee skirts for your legs (but nothing too short at the office). Opt for fitted jackets that hit at the hip line matched with flowing slacks in a dark color to camouflage a thick tummy. A sport jacket with a slight pattern will also help minimize a larger bust. Men's jackets should fall just below the widest part of the hip, and pants should have flat fronts with no flap pockets. A three-button jacket works well for taller men. Both men and women who are apples should avoid tight-fitting jeans and pleated pants.

▶ **Rectangle.** If you are a rectangle, you don't have many curves, and your body shape is more like a straight-up-and-down board. If this is your body type, do not wear clothes that are too clingy or fitted. Rectangular women should buy looser clothes that flow and give a semblance of curves. Halter styles are a good choice, as are fabrics in lighter shades near your shoulders and darker shades at your waist and hips, which create the illusion of a nipped-in waistline. You can also lengthen your silhouette with long cardigans, coats, and capes, or wear sheath dresses that fall in a straight (but not tight) line. Make sure to wear your tops untucked if you have a heavy waist, and pair them with slender, color-matched bottoms.

Men with a rectangular shape can wear clothes well, but they must be careful not to wear jackets that are too wide in the chest.

▶ **Pear.** Pear-shaped figures are smaller above the waist and larger below. The key for pear-shaped women is to draw attention to the upper half of your body—divert attention to north of the border. Boot-cut pants are perfect for pears, because they widen below the knee and flare out slightly at the bottom. The result is slimmer-looking thighs and hips. Make sure to buy pants that end before the waist begins. Lower-rise pants elongate the waist. For an even longer silhouette, wear boot-cut pants with shoes or boots that have a slight heel. Pears should also choose A-line skirts, which are both comfortable and flattering.

Horizontal necklines will make the top half of a woman's body look more balanced with the lower half. For a perfect match, pair these tops with dark-colored boot-cut trousers. For men, the key is to balance and call attention to your chest and away from your hips with a boat-neck sweater over a shirt. And while your first instinct might be to wear a jacket that is longer to hide the hips, your best bet is to make sure your jacket falls no lower than your hipbone. Wearing pleated pants is good for men with this kind of body shape.

There Is No Such Thing as Being Too Tall or Too Small

I can't say this enough: Whatever your body challenges are, and we all have them, the right clothing will help you enhance your assets and camouflage your flaws. With so many options on the market today, there is no need to hide in the closet. As I've mentioned before, the *Change One Thing* rule of thumb is to tackle your problem area first. In other words, if your shoulders are too broad, find the right garment that fits your shoulders first

▶ **ANNA'S REALITY CHECK** ▶▶

It is a rare person who can buy something off the rack and expect it to fit perfectly. This is why God invented tailors. You should have an experienced tailor take your measurements and alter your garments accordingly. Men already do this when they buy suits, but women need to make friends with a tailor as well.

before altering it to fit the rest of your body. If you are a full-figured woman, stay away from prints. Stick to subdued colors that won't make you look like a walking billboard. Big and tall men should avoid plaids or tweeds. Larger men sometimes think they need to wear baggy pants with a big break to hide their heft, when actually flat-front trousers will make them look slimmer. On the same note, big guys should choose a narrow rather than a wide tie to further slim down their image. I said narrow tie, not skinny. That went out with the vinyl record.

If you are a petite woman, the most important thing for you to do when selecting clothes is to pay attention to the length of your jacket and skirt. Petite women should wear a shorter jacket that doesn't go too far below the hips. I like shorter women to push the envelope a little bit and not be so proportionately correct, because they will look dated. Kelly Ripa of TV's "Regis and Kelly" is a good example of a petite celebrity who dresses stylishly for her size. She sometimes goes a little longer and a little wider, but it works. If you are small, your skirt should fall at the knee or an inch above. Do not go more than three inches above the knee for business attire.

If you have a large bust, fitted clothes can be flattering, but don't go too low with the cleavage. And all women, large or small, should get fitted for a bra. A well-fitted bra not only makes you look younger and perkier; it also won't pinch, cinch, or sag and give you those muffin rolls.

Typically, shorter men should not wear cuffs, but if you decide you want to wear them, make sure the cuff is proportionate to your height, and have pants made with a slight break. As for jacket length, a diminutive man, like a petite woman, should wear shorter jackets. You should be able to cup your fingers under your jacket, so if you can't touch the bottom, it's too long. And men, do not compensate for being vertically challenged by wearing a higher-heeled shoe. You will end up looking like John Travolta in *Saturday Night Fever*.

Ten "Will Powers" for Improving Body Image

You might not be able to change the body you were born with, but there are many things you can do to change your way of thinking about your body. To build your body confidence, try new activities, and find things you are comfortable doing at your current weight and fitness level. For every negative thought you have about your body, come up with a positive one to counter it. Try not to break your body down into parts, but think of yourself as a whole, functioning human being.

Psychologists Michael Levine, Ph.D., and Linda Smolak, Ph.D., came up with what they call ten "Will Powers" for improving your body image, which I want to share with you, in case you struggle with this issue. They suggest using "I will" affirmations because how we view our bodies is often inextricably linked with how we view ourselves. Here are their ten affirmations:

1. Twice a day, every day, I will ask myself, "Am I benefiting from focusing on what I believe are the flaws in my body weight or shape?"

2. I will think of three reasons why it is ridiculous for me to believe that thinner people are happier and "better." I will repeat these reasons to myself whenever I feel the urge to compare my body shape to someone else's.

3. I will spend less time in front of mirrors—especially when they are making me feel uncomfortable and self-conscious about my body.

4. I will exercise for the joy of feeling my body move and grow stronger and not simply to lose weight or "make up for" calories I have eaten.

5. I will participate in activities that I enjoy, even if they call attention to my weight and shape. I will constantly remind myself that I deserve to do things I enjoy, like dancing, swimming, etc., no matter what my shape or size.

6. I will refuse to wear clothes that are uncomfortable or that I do not like, but wear simply because they divert attention from my weight or shape. Instead, I will wear clothes that are comfortable and also right for my particular body shape.

7. I will list five to ten good qualities that I have, such as understanding, intelligence, or creativity. I will repeat these to myself whenever I start to feel bad about my body.

8. I will practice taking people seriously for what they say, feel, and do, not for how slender they appear.

9. I will surround myself with people and things that make me feel good about myself. When I'm around people and things that support me and make me feel good, I will be less likely to judge myself on the way my body looks.
10. I will treat my body with respect and kindness. I will feed it, keep it active, and listen to its needs. I will remember that my body is the vehicle that will carry me towards my dreams!

Get Rid of Your Inner Supermodel

The images we see in the media contribute greatly to the way we view our bodies, especially for women. We are constantly comparing ourselves with retouched or cosmetically altered people who are paraded before us on TV, in magazines, and on film. And the media's portrayal of what is "normal" keeps getting thinner for women and more muscle-bound for men. Twenty-five years ago, the average female model weighed 8 percent less than the average American woman. Today, a typical female model is 23 percent lighter. To a lesser extent, men are also being exposed to more images of guys who have gone from Joe Six-Pack to Joe Six-Pack Abs.

Looking at those perfectly shaped creatures called models only causes body angst or, worse, eating disorders. The body image problem among teenagers and young women is so bad that it has become a health issue. The research group Anorexia Nervosa and Related Eating Disorders says that one out of every four college-aged women in America uses unhealthy methods of weight control—including fasting, skipping meals, excessive exercise, laxative abuse, and self-induced vomiting. The pressure to be thin is also affecting young girls: in 2003, *Teen* magazine reported that 35 percent of girls 6 to 12 years old have been on at least one diet, and that 50 to 70 percent of normal-weight girls believe they are overweight.

So women, please don't let the media define what beauty is for you. I tell my clients who are struggling with body issues to go cold turkey on the fashion magazines and TV ads. Get rid of your inner supermodel by controlling what you see on any given day. If you don't want to take such drastic measures, at least tell yourself that what you are looking at isn't a reflection of reality. Most people are not celebrities who can work out ten hours a day with a personal trainer and afford expensive plastic surgery. They are like you and me—imperfect but beautiful in our own way!

Common Myths About Body Size

The National Association to Advance Fat Acceptance (NAAFA) believes that people should be able to live large without being discriminated against by a bunch of thin people. And while we know that being obese can increase our risk of diabetes and heart disease, being five or ten pounds overweight is certainly not a death sentence. If you happen to be a person of size, you might want to visit the NAAFA's website at www.naafa.org, where I found the following myths about weight.

Myth: *Fat people are ugly.*

Fact: Beauty is a learned concept, and the cultural norm of beauty changes over time. In the thirties, zaftig actress Mae West was considered a sex symbol, as was Marilyn Monroe in the fifties and sixties. Both would be considered "overweight" by today's standards. Keep in mind that the media, advertisers, and diet industry tend to set the standard of beauty for today's society.

Myth: *You have to exercise a lot for it to do any good, weight-wise.*

Fact: Because even the most vigorous exercise burns calories at a slower rate than most people consume them, weight loss is difficult to achieve and maintain without daily workouts. Yet there are other enormous health benefits to doing just thirty minutes of moderate activity (like walking) on most days, which can be broken up into ten minutes three times a day. And any movement is better than no movement. You could start with a five-minute walk today and build up from there.

Myth: *Fat people are lazy.*

Fact: Different people have different bodies. Sure, there might be some lazy fat people, but there are also plenty of lazy thin people. All of our bodies have a different natural baseline size, and while food intake and exercise may contribute to changing this, there are also many other factors involved that can't be controlled, such as metabolism, bone structure, and genetics. Just because some people are fat does not mean they are lazier than someone who is thinner.

Myth: *You can tell if someone has an eating disorder.*

Fact: There are many types of eating disorders, and they all manifest themselves differently. Many people with eating disorders are very good at hiding their eating and exercising habits.

People can be fat, thin, or somewhere in between and have an eating disorder. Even if they do not meet the medical criteria for size, weight, or behavior of an eating disorder, it does not mean that they do not need help. Eating disorders get worse as they go on, and it's even possible for people with an eating disorder to be unaware that they have a problem.

Myth: *Eating disorders are a woman's problem.*

Fact: Eating disorders affect many people regardless of gender, race, ethnicity, age, class, or sexual orientation. All types of eating disorders affect men as well as women, including anorexia, bulimia, compulsive overeating, and over-exercise. Due to the myth that eating disorders don't affect men, fewer men who have eating disorders have actually been labeled as such. Most figures say that about 10 percent of people with eating disorders in the United States are men, though even this number may be low.

Myth: *All fat people are compulsive overeaters.*

Fact: The compulsive eater, whether fat or thin, is a person with an eating disorder. Simply being fat does not indicate the presence of an eating disorder. Compulsive dieters, who ignore their body's hunger messages, tend to become obsessed with food and usually overeat after a round of dieting. Thyroid problems might also cause someone who does not overeat to be fat.

Weight and the Workplace

However you might feel about your body weight, studies have found that, when compared with job applicants with the same qualifications, obese job seekers are rated more negatively than average-weight people and are less likely to be hired. One reason for this disparity is that fat people are assumed to be lazier and unfit for meeting clients or the public. They are also thought to be less adept in supervisory positions and to have less self-discipline, poor personal hygiene, and lower ambition or productivity. Some companies have even flirted with the idea of charging overweight people unless they meet certain standards for weight, cholesterol, and blood pressure.

Obese women fare a bit worse than their male counterparts, according to a 2007 study of more than 2,800 Americans. In that study, more than 27 percent reported some kind of weight-based employment discrimination such as being passed over for promotions or being subject to derogatory remarks.

Only three cities—Washington, D.C., San Francisco, and Santa Cruz (California)—have laws against discriminating on the basis of weight, so there isn't much you can do legally if you don't live in those cities and you think you are a victim of weight bias. My best advice for you, aside from doing your best to get healthy by exercising and eating smaller, nutritionally balanced meals, is to dress according to your body type as I outlined earlier and convey confidence by concentrating on your areas of strength and ability to get the job done. If you are morbidly obese, it might be easier to find jobs where you don't deal as much with the public. Unfortunately, you might have to work harder to prove yourself, but prove yourself you must in order to stay competitive.

Mirror, Mirror

Researcher Kathleen Martin Ginis, an associate professor at McMaster University, in Hamilton, Ontario, discovered that it's easier for men who work out to notice and feel good about the changes in their bodies. Women, even those who are exercising and doing strength training, are far more self-critical and require concrete proof that their bodies are changing in order to feel good about themselves.

The 2003 university study conducted by Ginis followed men and women between the ages of 18 and 29 during a twelve-week full-body progressive strength-training program. Significant body image improvements were found for both sexes, but it seems that men's and women's body image improved for different reasons. For the men, body image improvements were related to perceived changes in their bodies. For the women, body image improvements were related to perceived and real changes in their bodies.

According to Ginis's study, men need only look at themselves in the mirror and see their belts going in a notch or two in order to feel good about their bodies. Women, however, required hard, physical evidence before they were able to improve their body image. The study found that men didn't base their positive body image on how much weight they lost or how much muscle they gained. Simply feeling stronger and more muscular and having their pants fit looser was enough to boost their body image. But when it came to the women, feeling thinner and stronger was only part of the story. They wanted the hard numbers on the scale.

If you are a woman who is struggling with your weight, please don't be a slave to your scale. Do what men do, and look at yourself in the mirror instead. Do you look any different than you did before you started exercising? Do you feel more energized and have more stamina to face your day-to-day activities? Are you able to lift heavier packages or carry your children without hurting your back? These are the kinds of litmus tests that we must all use to judge ourselves as we try to stay away from fad diets and those numbers on the scale. It's not how much you weigh; it's how you look, how you feel, and how you enjoy life that makes the difference.

Let Your Face Be the Star

One of the first things people should notice when they meet you is your eyes and face. Your clothes and hair aren't the stars; you are! Be careful not to create what I call a visual assault. Examples of visual assaults include huge, gaudy pins, garish nail polish, appliqués on sweaters, a wild beard, spiky or oddly colored hair, or lenses in glasses that are too thick. You get the picture, and it's not a pretty one.

One day when I was out to lunch with friends, I noticed a young Asian woman sitting at another table. The reason she stood out was not that she was beautiful, which she was, but that she had dyed her jet-black hair platinum blond. And if that wasn't jolting enough, she also wore bright pink lipstick. As an Asian woman myself, I know that this look is not a good one for us. There are better ways to get people to notice you.

The best thing you can wear on your face, aside from natural-looking makeup, is a friendly expression. Nothing is more inviting than someone with an engaging smile. One of my clients complained that the men she would meet at parties would ask her if she had just lost her best friend. This happened so frequently that she finally wanted to know why. After interviewing her, I discovered that she had some anger issues, which she unwittingly displayed in her facial expression. The corners of her mouth turned down, and her eyebrows were knotted into a permanent grimace. She needed to learn how to smile.

In addition to doing something like yoga to help her to breathe and relax, I suggested she practice smiling in the mirror until it became more natural to her. I told her to think about someone or something that made her happy, such as a child, a pet, or a funny experience. It helps if you smile on the inside, but faking it at first is OK. She didn't change overnight, but eventually she started smiling more, and her social life picked up as soon as she learned how to put on a happier face.

If you think you may be a frowner, have someone record a video of you in a social setting, and when you watch it, pay attention to your expression. It might be a rude awakening, but I can't emphasize enough the importance of having a pleasant facial expression. It will change the tenor of every interaction. Enlist a friend to gently tap you on the shoulder whenever you start to grimace. As I said in my introduction, I had to teach myself to smile more often when I gave presentations so I didn't seem so intimidating. I had no idea how I was coming across to others until I watched a video of myself giving a speech.

The Truth About Plastic Surgery

Now that cosmetic surgery has come out of the closet and become as commonplace as bridgework, clients frequently ask me whether or not they should go under the knife (or laser). Here's my opinion about plastic surgery in a nutshell: It depends on what procedure you are considering and the physical and emotional benefit it will bring you.

Think of the skin on your face as drapes that have been hanging up for thirty-plus years and exposed to sun and hot and cold temperatures. When you take them to the cleaners, the clerk tells you the cleaners cannot guarantee what will happen when they are cleaned. It's the same as for your skin. There is no guarantee. My number one criterion for plastic surgery is that it should make you look the same, only better.

As Charla Krupp wrote in her great book *How Not to Look Old*, the last thing you want is to look like you've had too much work done. Think of the celebrities who have had too much work, like Meg Ryan and, heaven help him, Michael Jackson. To a far lesser extent, Jennifer Grey (*Dirty Dancing*) admits that she lost some of her character after her nose job, which made her look cute but ultimately generic—robbing her of the quirky charm that landed her many of her key roles in the first place. The poster celeb for good cosmetic work is Demi Moore. She looks as if she has been frozen in time, but her face doesn't look as if it has been frozen by dry ice. An overly Botoxed face will be immobile, and being able to smile is far more important that having a creaseless face.

The goal of any cosmetic procedure is a moderate and natural enhancement. So you might want to opt for a simple eye lift to remove excess baggage or Fraxel laser treatments that smooth out the skin gradually over a period of several months. Breast enhancements are fine as long as they are not overdone (think Pamela Anderson), and can even help your clothing fit better. The same goes for breast reductions, which can also help get rid of back pain. I'm also all for operations to reduce varicose veins, which last for twenty years and can make a difference in both your health and appearance.

Keep in mind that none of these procedures are cheap or foolproof. If you can afford plastic surgery, make sure you go to a physician who has been recommended by someone you know. Also, do some research to see if the doctor is board certified in his or her field.

Hair Transplants

The days of comb-overs and toupees (who are you fooling?) are over, thanks to the bald-is-beautiful movement. Go to my website (www.personalimagesinc.com) to see my Fox TV appearance on comb-overs.

The best option for men who are in recession is to shave it all off or go closely cropped like actors Bruce Willis or Patrick Stewart. If that doesn't suit your pate, then hair transplants where you can't see the plugs are another option. William Shatner ("Star Trek," "Boston Legal") has a good transplant.

4

WHAT KIND OF COLLEAGUE ARE YOU?

Change One Thing About Your Business Style

▶▶ WHEN I TALK about your office image, I'm referring to how you see yourself and how others see you when you are at work. Are you a perfectionist or a slacker? A taskmaster or a pushover? A blamer or a sharer? A leader or a follower? In these difficult economic times, companies are constantly looking for ways to skim the fat, so you need to be especially aware of the image you are projecting at work. Remember, no one is indispensable, from the person who delivers the mail to the person who cuts your check.

What's Your Work Style?

Communications expert Tony Alessandra, Ph.D., came up with a great way to assess the four basic work styles, which I frequently use in my workshops. Keep in mind that you can have a combination of styles, but when push comes to shove, one of these will emerge before the others. Once you figure out which one best describes you in the workplace, you can use this information to adapt your style to the people you work with. It will make meetings run smoother, especially in negotiations, and it will help you with your personal as well as professional relationships.

Take the following business image quiz to determine your work style and see what you need to change in order to safeguard your job or improve your chances of getting a promotion.

▶▶ ANSWER TRUE OR FALSE:

1. My colleagues' feelings are important to me.
2. Getting a job done on time is more important than getting it all done correctly.
3. Having the data to support my results is essential.
4. It is more important to have a vision for a project than to have a strategy.
5. I like to be challenged by taking on new projects.
6. I enjoy being on a team more than leading a team.
7. I am good at remembering details.
8. I am comfortable changing direction with a project if it's not succeeding.
9. I seldom say anything I will regret.
10. I am afraid of failing when I start a new project.
11. I have no problem asking questions in a meeting.

12. Many people tell me I'm charming.
13. I am patient when a team member fails to fulfill his or her responsibility.
14. I like time before I make a decision.
15. I always try to find out the cause of a problem before I confront it.
16. People like being with me.
17. I like change.
18. I hate being put on the spot in a meeting.
19. When people meet me for the first time, they know I am the team leader.
20. I always send out an agenda before a meeting.
21. I hate confrontations.
22. I like to analyze all situations.
23. I like to get to know someone before I work with him or her.

Answers:

The Director. If you responded True to statements 2, 5, 8, 9, 19, and 20, you are a Director. Directors are goal oriented. They speak quickly and have high energy. The Director likes to run the show and can be abrupt. Directors have little patience for other people's ideas. If you work with a Director, you should keep your relationship businesslike and be supportive. Be careful not to take disagreements personally, and argue the facts—keep your emotions out of it.

The Relater. If you responded True to statements 1, 6, 13, 15, 18, and 21, you are a Relater. The Relater is a good consensus builder and a good listener. Relaters are more laid-back and rarely put their stakes in the ground. A Relater does not like to be told what to do and will probably clash with a Director. If you work with Relaters, it's a good idea to show support for their feelings and concerns. Show that you are listening to them, and be warm and sincere.

The Socializer. If you responded True to statements 4, 11, 12, 16, 17, and 23, you are a Socializer. Socializers are outgoing and fun to be around. They tend to be creative and excellent visionaries but are not as good at getting the job done. If you work with Socializers, try not to argue with them, and do not try to hurry along a discussion. Be supportive, entertaining, and keep your own record of any goals that need to be accomplished.

The Thinker. If you responded True to statements 3, 7, 10, 14, and 22, you are a Thinker. The Thinker is very process and data driven. Thinkers are not creative and do not like to take risks. Thinkers like to go over the details before making a move and do not work well with Relaters or Socializers. To work well with a Thinker, you must be systematic, organized, and well prepared. List both the pros and cons of any plan, and demonstrate understanding through action rather than words.

Anna's Business Image Tips

The following tips are rules of thumb that everyone, regardless of business style, would do well to heed!

Never Burn a Bridge—You Might Need to Cross It Again Someday

Most of us have worked with someone whom we feel has done us wrong. When this happens, we may naturally react by feeling angry, self-righteous, or victimized. This is especially true if you are fired or laid off. No matter how angry or hurt you might feel at the time, take a deep breath, and try not to react defensively. Don't threaten or bad-mouth the company or person who fired you. The decision has already been made. Should you have an exit interview, it's OK to give constructive criticism about how you think your position or department could have been managed better. It won't help you, but it might help your former coworkers or the next person who takes your place. Taking the high road might get you a good reference letter or some leads for your next job.

When I was selling real estate, I helped a friend by showing him a home that he fell in love with. He ended up buying the house without telling me, so I lost thousands of dollars in commission fees. I never said anything to him about it, but I ended our friendship immediately because I was unable to forgive what I saw as his betrayal. This man later became the CEO of a major corporation that I wanted to have as a client.

What I should have done, had I been a more mature businesswoman, was to tell him that I was disappointed that he bought the house without me but hoped he would come to me the next time he wanted to purchase real estate. You never know when you might cross paths again with those you've had disagreements with. I am not suggesting that you forgive all injustices, but be aware that, as the Disney song reminds us, the world is smaller than you think.

Swim Away from the Sharks

Every situation has its "sharks"—people who will do whatever it takes and step on whomever they need to in order to advance their career or self-interest. Most sharks are never happy, because they are always climbing and there are always people who get in their way. If you've been in business for more than a minute, you've probably met a shark.

You have two choices when you encounter sharks. You can fight them, or you can swim away and observe them from a safe distance. If you decide to do battle with a shark, you run the risk of being eaten alive. Sharks are usually that good. If you choose to watch them closely, you might learn from them. I'm not suggesting that you copy their ruthlessness, but they probably have some skills that will help you in the future. Is there something they are doing that would work for you? I know it's not easy, but try to change your attitude about sharks. Don't get defensive if they say or do something that makes you angry. Remember, sharks can smell blood from miles away, so behaving frantically around sharks will only make them more determined to destroy you. Observe, learn, and swim away!

Making Your Partner Look Good Is the Key to a Successful Career

One of the exercises in the Second City Improv Workshops I took was doing scenes with a partner. By working one-on-one with another performer, we learned that the key to a successful comedy skit is not just highlighting yourself, but making your fellow actor look good. It should not be about trying to upstage your partner; it should be about working as a team or as an ensemble. Sometimes you throw your partner a line that you know he or she will use to get a laugh and vice versa. Talk show hosts do this all the time. They set up their guests by asking them a question that will lead to a funny or interesting anecdote. By playing the straight man or woman, they allow their guests to shine, and everyone ends up looking good.

It is the same in the business world. Should someone on your team forget to bring an important handout to a meeting, for example, never embarrass him or her in front of others. Do your best to fill in for the forgetful person and smooth over the gaffe. Being a team player is one of the most important skills one can develop in business, because it builds trust and shows that you know when to put the company's best interest ahead of your own.

Do You Have Bad Work Habits?

Are you having trouble getting along with your coworkers? Are you being passed over for promotions? If so, you might want to check to see if you are doing something at work that is putting people off. The following eleven work habits are the most annoying ones that I hear about in my workshops. If you do any of these things, it's time to break yourself of your bad behavior, so you will have a better chance of moving up instead of out.

1. You snap your gum. You might not realize it if you like to chew gum, but snapping is extremely annoying to those around you. In addition to being unattractive, gum snapping and bubble popping are up there with whistling, finger tapping, and humming on the scale of annoying habits. Unless you have a private office, do not snap, crackle, or pop at work.

2. You smell. If you think you might stink but aren't sure, ask a friend or relative to tell you the truth. Some people sweat a lot, so make sure that you shower often and use deodorant if this applies to you. Smokers, although banned from indulging in the office, still carry the smell of smoke long after they have come back from their break. If you must smoke, do it outside where your clothes can air out as much as possible, or have a "smoking jacket," an article of clothing that you wear while smoking and leave in the closet afterward. And go easy on the fragrances. Many people are allergic to perfume, cologne, and aftershave, so wearing too much, which means the fragrance hangs in the air long after you've left the room, will make people want to strap on an oxygen mask.

3. You talk too loudly on the phone. Unless you have a private office, use your indoor voice when talking on the phone. This is one of the complaints I hear most often from office workers, especially those who are sitting side by side in cubicles.

4. You goof off too much. Everyone goofs off now and then, which is fine and actually good for recharging the batteries. Companies like Google encourage letting off steam by having basketball courts and Ping Pong tables at the office, because they know that workers will stay at the office longer when they are having fun. But if you are missing deadlines and are more of an online poker player than a team player, your colleagues (and supervisors) will soon tire of your all-play-and-no-work attitude.

5. You're a brownnoser. While it's important to stay in the good graces of your boss, kissing up to the supervisor is not only irritating, it's also counterproductive. Business leaders don't need or want people who agree with everything they say, because they are not always right. Having an original thought and coming up with new and better ideas is far better for the company. Staying later than everyone else on your team so you can e-mail the boss with a time stamp to give the impression that you were last man or woman standing is another example of a grandstanding ploy that will backfire. Remember, it is just as important to be considered a team player and to have the respect of your colleagues as it is to be the apple of your supervisor's eye.

6. You are always late. Everyone is late once in a while, whether it's the result of being caught behind a slow-moving truck, being delayed by a sick passenger on the train, or having a child miss the school bus. But chronically late people who are constantly coming up with excuses for their tardiness or simply waltzing into work well past the expected arrival time show that they just don't care enough about their job. Johnny- and Jane-come-latelies need to set their alarm clocks twenty minutes ahead to give themselves some wiggle room, should unforeseen circumstances arise. It's less stressful for everyone, including you. Successful folks manage their time; time does not manage them.

7. You're unprepared. Unless you work for yourself, you must be a team player, which means you are required to do whatever is necessary to hold up your end. Just because you cheated off of someone else's paper when you were in college doesn't mean you should depend on others to do your work for you. Being unprepared at a meeting is embarrassing for you and, ultimately, reflects badly on the entire company.

8. You're a blamer. There is always someone who believes or pretends that he or she is never wrong. These annoying people are continually looking for scapegoats and covering their tracks so they appear to have a spotless record. If you have a tendency to point the finger at others when you make a mistake, you will eventually lose all credibility and be universally despised. Everyone makes mistakes, so own up to it by learning from them and saying, "My bad, but it won't happen again."

9. You're two-faced. If you smile and act friendly to someone's face and then turn around and bad-mouth the person to others behind his or her back, then you are the classic two-face. You probably don't even realize you are doing it, which makes this bad work habit one of the most insidious. If you have a beef with someone you work with, see that person privately, and air out your differences. Pretending to form an alliance with someone when you want nothing more than to bring the person down is behavior worthy of a cheesy reality show—and doesn't belong in the workplace.

10. You're an office squatter. This far less nefarious but equally annoying habit involves taking up residence in a coworker's office and overstaying your welcome. A simple way to correct this problem is to ask, "Are you busy?" or, "Do you have some time to chat?" before you sit down. It gives people an opportunity to say they can't talk now but will call you later when they are free. Some people are too polite to ask you to scram.

11. You're a Drama Queen. Drama Queens know no gender or sexual orientation. They thrive in a crisis, real or imagined, and turn the smallest infraction into a meltdown. Everything must revolve around them, or else they will manufacture a reason to be the center of attention. If this sounds like you, heed the advice of any savvy elementary-school kid, and save the drama for your mama!

When It's Time to Change Jobs

Despite our best efforts to change situations for the better, sometimes the best way to save our health and sanity is to quit. If the economy is in the Dumpster, you might have to wait for an uptick, but that doesn't mean you can't start polishing up your résumé.

How do you know when the time has come to go? Take an inventory of your misery index in order to determine if you should rev up your job search engines. Unless you have some kind of financial cushion, do not quit until you get another job. Here are some signs that it's time to pull out the interview suit:

▶ **You get sick to your stomach every Sunday.** If you continually feel nauseated on Sunday evening just *thinking* about going back to work, start putting out feelers for another job. Your physical and mental well-being is more important than your career, and being in a constant state of stress can be hazardous to your health.

▶ **The work environment is toxic.** Has the morale at your office hit rock bottom? Does everyone walk on eggshells because the boss is a sadistic screamer? Are coworkers so obnoxious or evil that you are taking breaks every fifteen minutes in order to breathe the precious air of freedom? Toxic work environments can be tolerated for short periods, but eventually everyone will go belly up if they stay too long. If you are being harassed sexually or psychologically, report the offenders to human resources immediately. You might get a settlement to take with you on your way out the door.

▶ **You're doing the work of ten people.** With the increased numbers of layoffs, companies are depending on workers who remain to pick up the slack for downsized employees for no additional money. According to CareerBuilder.com, 68 percent of workers feel burnout at work, and 45 percent describe their workloads as too heavy. If all you have the energy to do when you get home is watch back-to-back TV shows with a micro-waved dinner, it's time to send out your résumé.

▶ **It's been years since your last raise or promotion.** If five or ten years have passed without a change in the numbers in your paycheck and you've been working your heart out, doing a great job, and have asked for a raise several times to no avail, you are not being respected at work. The same goes for a promotion and title bump, which can increase your value in the marketplace even if you are being undervalued financially at your current position. Loyalty is not always rewarded these days, so get out there and see what you are really worth!

▶ **You are being shut out.** Are you being left out of important meetings? Missing the memos that are being circulated to people on your team? Are you never asked to join your coworkers for lunch? It's not hard to see when you are being shut out, and that's a major red flag that you are being set up for a fall.

▶ **You are about to be laid off.** By the time you hear rumors that the company is going to be downsizing or is about to outsource your job to India, it's probably true. Get on the horn, fire out some e-mails, and start networking for another job.

▶ **You're bored.** While there are worse things in life than being bored, consider that you are spending forty hours a week at work, which is a lot of time if you are clock-watching or checking YouTube and blogs for the latest post. You don't necessarily have to quit, but you might want to change something about your job to make it more challenging and interesting. Ask your boss if you can take on more responsibility or learn a new skill at a local college.

Career Change Caveats

If you decide it's time to change gears by changing careers, remember to look around before you leap. Unless you are independently wealthy or have enough of a nest egg to support yourself during the search process, don't quit before you have a solid offer. As miserable as you might feel now, knowing that you are actively networking, scouring job sites, registering with recruiters, and doing your research (including reading books like this one) should make you feel better. Here are some other caveats to keep in mind during your job search:

▶ **Don't take the first available job.** When your job misery index is high, you might be tempted to grab the first opening you find. Make sure that you investigate the new position by talking to people who currently work at the company you are interviewing with and those who have worked there in the past. The last thing you want to do is to move from one bad job to another.

▶ **Don't be afraid to change fields.** Sure, it's scary to go in a completely new direction after spending years in your current field, but you will never be fulfilled in your career if you stay

▶ FASTEST-GROWING CAREERS ▶▶▶

Whether you are considering a job change or just starting out, here's some information that might help guide your choices. The following are the five fastest-growing careers, according to the latest U.S. Bureau of Labor Statistics projections, which appeared in *Newsday*:

Personal and home-care aides
2006 employment: 767,000
2016 projection: 1,156,000
Salary: $21,220 or less

Network systems and data communications analysts
2006 employment: 262,000
2016 projection: 402,000
Salary: $46,360 and up

Veterinarians
2006 employment: 62,000
2016 projection: 84,000
Salary: $46,360 and up

Skin-care specialists
2006 employment: 38,000
2016 projection: 51,000
Salary range: $21,260–$30,560

Makeup artists, theatrical, and performance
2006 employment: 2,000
2016 projection: 3,000
Salary: $30,630–$46,300

in an industry that you dislike or are thoroughly bored with. I know it's not easy, and it will take some time to navigate the learning curve, but sometimes shaking things up is necessary.

▶ **Don't necessarily go with the highest bidder.** While money is certainly a factor in choosing a job, it shouldn't be your only consideration. You can't put a price on job satisfaction, so if a big paycheck also means working late every night and on weekends and you would like to spend some more time with your kids, you might want to trade the money for your life.

▶ **Don't go back to school until you know what you want to do next.** My coauthor, Jodie, knew someone who wanted to change her career from a medical journalist to a doctor. She quit her job and was accepted to Harvard, where she needed to take pre-med courses *before* going to the med school. Several years and tens of thousands of dollars later, she decided dissecting cadavers wasn't for her. Now she has school loans to repay, and she's back to doing medical writing. The moral of this story is, don't invest your time and money in tuition before you are absolutely sure about what you want to do next. You can always start by volunteering or doing an internship in a new field so you can get some on-the-job experience first.

Do You Have a Negative Work Image?

Is something that is going on at work giving you a negative work image? If so, it's time to change whatever is holding you back, so you don't risk being on the short list for layoffs. Here are some common office obstacles, as well as strategies for breaking down those barriers to success:

▶ **You don't get enough face time with the boss.** Do you see your boss only during group meetings or while washing your hands in the rest room? Having too little face time with the boss can be disastrous for your career, because being "what's-her-face" means you are a persona non grata at your company.

Quick-fix change: It's OK to ask for meetings with your boss to discuss what you are doing at work and to ask questions if you need guidance. If your supervisor is too busy for an office chat, send a memo or e-mail with a status report and a note saying you are available to discuss the issue at his or her convenience. Making small talk in the elevator also is a good way to open up the lines of communication.

▶ **You're the new kid on the block.** Being a newbie is difficult, because you are not yet comfortable with the corporate culture or office politics. There's a learning curve for all new employees, so it will take some time before you earn the trust and confidence of your coworkers and are considered one of the gang.

Quick-fix change: After figuring out where the supply room is, try to learn everyone's name and title. Don't be afraid to ask questions if you don't know something, and try to find a person who will mentor you until you get the hang of things. Invite a coworker out of lunch to pick his or her brain and get the inside scoop on who's the shark and who's the starfish.

▶ **Your work area is a mess.** Not everyone is organized by nature, but if you have a filing system that only you can under-stand, the next time you are out sick and someone is trying to find an important document on your mile-high pile, you will be cursed by your coworkers.

Quick-fix change: Instead of being known as the office slob, take time at the end of each work day to organize your work-space or office. Make use of files, folders, boxes, or binders that are clearly marked so others can identify them as well. In these increasingly paperless times, do the same for your computer files. Make folders and put labeled documents in them, so others can retrieve them easily.

▶ **You work alone most of the time.** Some jobs involve hours spent alone in front of a computer or assignments that don't require working as a team. If you are one of those people who fly solo at work, you are missing out on the camaraderie of coworkers and, even worse, are likely to be forgotten or passed over for raises or promotions.

Quick-fix change: Request to be included on the next group project, or ask for someone to bounce your ideas off of. If there is no opportunity to join forces in your day-to-day job, join the softball team or some other after-work activity where you have a chance to mix and mingle.

▶ **Nobody listens to you.** Are your ideas not being heard or respected? Do you feel as though you know exactly how to fix a problem at work but no one is listening?

Quick-fix change: Some people speak more forcefully than others, which is why the meek are unlikely to inherit the com-pany. Practice being more assertive (without being aggressive) by following up if you are not being heard. Use the power words listed in the communication chapter (Chapter 6), make eye con-tact when you are presenting an idea, and be persistent without being a pest.

Little White Lies That Backfire

No one is 100 percent honest all of the time, especially in the workplace. Besides, it's not always to our advantage to tell the truth when a little white lie might help us save time, save face, or save our necks. That said, there are times when honesty is the best business policy, such as when you are asked the following questions:

▶ **Do you have any questions?** If you are unsure about an assignment or task and are asked if you have any questions, do not be afraid to speak up. While, contrary to popular belief, there *is* such a thing as a stupid question, it is better to ask than to try muddling through in the dark.

▶ **Can you do this for me?** When a deadline is approaching and a boss or coworker asks you if you can take on more work, do not say, "Sure, no problem," when you want to say, "Are you kidding me?" Politely but firmly say, "I'm sorry, but I'm on deadline, and I'm up to my ears already. Maybe [*insert coworker's name*] can help." You can also tell the person asking you for help that you will see if your deadline can be moved. If not, you will at least get points for trying.

▶ **Why were you late?** Everyone is late once in a while, so resist the temptation to make up a story like "My alarm didn't go off" or "My kid got sick this morning," if you lost track of time. A simple "Sorry" before getting right down to work will suffice.

▶ **Are you sick?** Do not come to work when you are sick! Sneezing, wheezing, and coughing all over your coworkers is not only annoying, it will spread your germs. Don't be a martyr; stay in bed until you are better.

▶ **Are you almost finished with the project?** Do not say you are on schedule with a project if you haven't started it yet or if you know for certain that you will need at least another day to finish. Let your supervisor know that you are running behind, so he or she can either get you some help or push the deadline back if possible.

Use Your Annual Review as an Instrument for Change

Many workers fear their annual review because they feel they must defend their performance when criticized. Try not to look at your review as a trial by fire. Instead, look at it as an opportunity to make your case for a promotion or raise. Keep a list of your achievements, including the date performed and how each achievement directly or indirectly helped the company's bottom line. Bring that list with you to the review, so you are well armed to present documented instances where you have gone above and beyond your job description. Job reviews also give you a chance to let your supervisor know what your goals are, including educational opportunities that the company might be willing to finance.

Here are some other ways you can prepare for your review:

▶ **Review your job description.** Go over the job description given to you by the human resources department, so you are reminded of everything you are supposed to do.

▶ **Do a self-review.** Many managers will ask you to critique your strengths and weaknesses, so be prepared to come up with examples of both. As in a job interview, you should select a weakness that can be overcome and be ready with solutions for how to improve. Refer to your success journal to document your achievements over the past year.

▶ **Tie up any loose ends.** If you have a project that is still unfinished, try to complete it before your review. If that isn't possible, select projects that you completed successfully in the past to use as examples of how you saw something through from start to finish.

▶ **Do not lie or cover up mistakes.** Any boss worth his or her salt is well aware of employee gaffes, so don't try to cover up your past mistakes. Own up to them, and explain what you learned from the experience and how you think similar mistakes could be avoided in the future.

▶ **Take notes.** Take copious notes on what your supervisor is saying, so you can refer to them in the future. You should also take a list of talking points that you would like to discuss after you have patiently listened to your boss and recorded the feedback.

▶ **Review the reviewer.** Annual reviews can swing both ways. They give you a chance to voice your opinions on how you think your department or company could improve, or ways that your boss could help make your job easier. This is not the place for a gripe session, so make sure your critiques are couched in positive way. For example, you could say, "I know you are busy with department head meetings, but it would be helpful if I could meet with you briefly once a week to give you a status report on the project I'm working on."

Are You a Bad Boss?

Many bosses are not aware of their failings. They might be good at giving job reviews to the people they manage, but not as good at asking, "How am I doing?" Knowing what the people you supervise think of your managerial skills can make you a better boss and make your team happier and more loyal. In Shakespeare's portrayal of the heroic Henry V of England, the king went undercover as one of his soldiers in order to see what his men really thought about his leadership skills. His band of happy warriors went on to win the battle against France. Need I say more?

Here are some bad boss behaviors to look out for:

▶ **You treat your assistant like a servant.** In the bestselling roman à clef *The Devil Wears Prada*, the evil editor of a powerful fashion magazine expected her assistant to hang up her coat, fetch her food and snacks, and run personal errands for her 24/7. While we understand that young up-and-comers must pay their dues, treating someone like a servant will engender untold anger and resentment that will spread like a viral video throughout the company. Plus, your poor indentured assistant will probably last only a few months before tiring of your imperious behavior, and training new people takes time and energy away from your work.

▶ **You never say, "Good job!"** Bosses whose parents never told them they were proud of them after a job well done are often doomed to pass along this tough-love MO when they are at the helm. It's fine to have high expectations, but when you only punish the bad without ever rewarding the good, you will have disaffected and resentful underlings. Being overly critical also puts the kibosh on creativity or initiative, because people live in fear of making mistakes. Try to remember to give credit for a job well done, so you don't break the spirits of those around you. Only a sadist enjoys watching employees collapse in a puddle of tears.

▶ **THE LATEST UN-NETWORKING TREND** ▶▶▶

I talk a lot about networking, which is essential for any businessperson, but if you're under 40 and work in a nontraditional or creative field like technology, design, advertising, or art, you might want to try something called Likemind instead. Many young professionals who don't wear suits to work are replacing the old-school shake-and-make for casual chat-and-chews at a local coffee house. These gatherings involve brainstorming, relationship building, and partner hunting and are taking place each month in fifty-five cities around the world, including, São Paulo, Shanghai, and Melbourne. They are the equivalent to the "unconference"—those unconventional, mostly geeky gatherings that have tried to replace the luxury-hotel executive retreat of the past. If there isn't a Likemind group in your town or city, start one up! For more information on Likemind networking groups in your area, go to www.likemind.us.

▶ **You're a screamer.** While yelling might help you let off some steam, it is downright humiliating to be on the receiving end of a tirade. If you are a screamer, take a break to calm down before dressing down the person at fault, or take an anger management course if taking deep breaths and counting to twenty don't do the trick.

▶ **You don't give instructions.** When managers are busy, they don't always want to take the time to give explicit directions about what they want their staff to do. Don't expect people to read your mind. Taking a few minutes to calmly explain what you want people to accomplish will save you time in the long run, because you won't have to go back and fix mistakes.

▶ **You hog all the credit.** It might sound like a cliché, but if you surround yourself with people who are as smart as or smarter than you are, you will end up looking like a genius, or at least someone who knows how to pick talent. But what's important is that you make sure those people get credit for their ideas and successes. Otherwise, they won't stick around long.

Networking Exercise: Your Thirty- to Sixty-Second Commercial

When you are networking, it is absolutely crucial that you be able to introduce yourself and explain what you do in thirty to sixty seconds. These self-promotional sound bites will let people know who you are and what you can do for them or for their business, which is the purpose of any networking situation or event. Fill in the following worksheet to help formulate your commercial.

My name is ————————————————————————————.

The company I work for is ——————————————————.

My title is —————————————————————————————.

My latest product/service/program is ————————————
——.

My customers or clients are ————————————————————
——.

What need or problem does your business address? ————————
——.

How does your business or service work? ——————————
——.

What distinguishes you from others? ——————————————
——.

I/my company have/has won ———————————— awards and citations.

My accomplishments include ————————————————————
——
——.

What *Not* to Talk About at a Networking Event

Certain subjects are off-limits at networking events. Remember, you are not there to meet your soul mate; you are there to get a job or recommendation. Here are some topics to avoid:

▶ **Religion.** People's spiritual beliefs are extremely personal, so don't risk saying something that might offend someone by talking about religion. This includes such controversial topics as intelligent design, cloning, abortion, stem cell research, and gay marriage. Wars have been started over less.

▶ **Politics.** While politics can be a fun topic to discuss among friends, stay away from political issues with people you've just met. As with religion, people take their political opinions quite seriously, so a pleasant conversation can easily turn ugly when people start making political statements. In a recent poll of users of Monster, a career search website, more than 26,000 respondents said that when it comes to talking politics with coworkers, "don't ask, don't tell" is the best policy. Forty-six percent said the best way to deal with political discussions is to "listen, but keep your opinions to yourself." I agree 100 percent.

▶ **Diet.** People who have weight issues, whether they are overweight or anorexic, tend to be sensitive about their size, so don't volunteer the fact that you lost twenty-five pounds on a grapefruit diet. Unless someone asks you how you stay so fit, don't talk about diets or food regimens with people you don't already know well.

▶ **Money.** Many of us were taught by our parents that it is impolite to talk about money. This rule holds true in networking situations. If someone compliments you about an item of clothing or jewelry, do not say, "Oh, I got this thing at a yard sale," or "Thank you; it cost me $200, which I thought was a bargain." Don't attach a monetary value to things, lest you appear materialistic or parsimonious.

▶ **Illness.** Networking events are not the place to discuss illnesses, so avoid this topic like the, um, plague. No one wants to hear about your colonoscopy over cocktails and hors d'oeuvres.

▶ **Marital status.** Keep in mind that you are at a business event, not a singles mixer, so do not ask if a person is married. Women, especially, will feel uncomfortable if this is raised by men, because they won't know whether or not they are being hit on. If a person mentions his or her spouse, then you can discuss the topic, if you wish.

▶ **Work gossip.** Don't spread rumors about people or internal company information. You shouldn't do this as a general rule, because gossip reflects badly on the person who's spreading it, and you don't want to be thought of as someone who can't be confided in or trusted.

Anna's Better Networking Tips

Here are a few of my favorite techniques, guaranteed to make any networking event work for you:

▶ **Come prepared with conversation starters.** You should have an opening line or two that will serve as an icebreaker when you approach someone you are meeting for the first time. Ice-breakers include "How did you hear about this event?" The way people respond will give you an idea of whether or not they are open to a conversation with you.

▶ **Look for a threesome.** If you don't know anyone, start by joining a group of three or more. Two people talking together might be engaged in a private conversation that they don't want interrupted. You can also approach the host of the event, who will introduce you to others, or simply someone with a friendly face.

▶ **Don't be afraid of small talk.** Suggested topics of conversation at parties and networking events include your latest travel adventures, recommendations for good local restaurants, movies that you enjoyed, good books that you've read, sports, the latest technological gadget or breakthrough, and current events, if positive.

▶ **Know what you are looking for before you start.** It's a waste of your time and others' if you go to a networking event before you know what kinds of jobs or companies you are looking for. Take time to do the exercises and take the quizzes in this book if you are not sure about what your next step should be.

▶ **Do your research.** Most people like to help, but they get weary when they are asked questions that can be answered by a simple Google search. Do your research before you start networking, so you sound informed.

▶ **Don't act desperate.** As hard as times might be, don't let on that your next mortgage payment depends on your getting a job yesterday. As when you're dating, people don't want to be with (or hire) anyone who sounds or acts desperate.

▶ **Don't do all the talking.** When networking with someone who can help you with leads to a job, make sure you are not the one doing all the talking. While it's important to let your mentor know about your skills, qualifications, and goals, the reason you are there is to gather as much information as possible from others.

▶ **Don't overstay your welcome.** Sure, people like to help others in need, which is what mentors do when they take you under their wing, but don't take advantage of their largesse by calling or e-mailing them every day with questions.

▶ **Ask before you name-drop.** Before you use the name of a contact you chatted up at a networking event, be sure you have gotten their permission to do so, or your name-dropping will come back to haunt you.

▶ **Don't come on too strong.** While it's great to project confidence in yourself and your expertise, be careful not to come on too strong while networking. There is a happy medium between self-assurance and shameless self-promotion—and the latter will often make the other party uncomfortable.

▶ **Don't forget the thank-you note.** Good networkers remember to thank the people who help them, so send a follow-up e-mail or note to the person you met, reminding him or her of your conversation and, above all, expressing thanks for his or her time and support.

NO WALLFLOWERS ALLOWED

Change One Thing About
Your Social Image

▶▶ WE ARE NOT born knowing the right thing to say, the right thing to wear, and the right way to behave. That knowledge starts with our parents, who teach us how to talk, share, and become good citizens of the world. Understanding proper etiquette is not just about what fork to use or about what to wear at a function. It's about making other people around you feel more comfortable.

What would you do if you were out at dinner party, for example, and the person next to you took your water glass by mistake? Would you turn to that person and say, "Hey, that's *my* water glass," or would you discreetly call the waiter over and say, "May I have another water glass, please"? Many people are afraid of making a social faux pas but do not realize that making others feel bad is the ultimate in bad form—far worse, and more common, than bad table manners. In contrast, when you do something nice for someone else, I guarantee that your kindness will be remembered. Whether that person is a business colleague or personal acquaintance, every kind act is an emotional deposit in the person that you can draw from in the future.

When it comes to socializing with coworkers or clients, knowing the proper protocol is even more difficult. Whom do you introduce first? When is it OK to give out your business card? Should you call the CEO by his or her first name? Do you clam up when more than two people are in a room?

The following business protocol quiz will tell you how much you know about business protocol, and the answers will help you shine like a polished professional whenever you mix business with pleasure.

▶▶ ANSWER TRUE OR FALSE:

1. Meeting with my clients socially is not necessary, because they know I am a busy person.
2. I know the difference between playing at a public golf course and at a country club.
3. When I'm traveling on business to a foreign country, I am aware of other people's cultural differences.
4. I always carry business cards.
5. I never offer a business card unless I am asked for one.
6. I always keep my right hand free to shake hands at a business function.
7. I never go back to the buffet table more than once at a business function.

8. I never leave someone I've just met at a party standing alone.

9. If a businessperson is a peer, I can call that person by his or her first name.

10. I always address an elderly person as Mr. or Ms. unless the person tells me otherwise.

11. When introducing people at work, I say the highest-level person's name first.

12. Business discussions during a luncheon should begin immediately after everyone is seated.

13. The purpose of a breakfast meeting is to discuss business.

14. I network at least once a month.

15. Posting a video of myself on YouTube is a great way to promote myself.

16. Men should always pick up the check, even if the boss is a woman.

17. When I take a client out to lunch or dinner, I like to try new restaurants.

Answers:

Use these answers to see what you need to change when you are socializing with coworkers or clients.

1. *False.* It is important to entertain business associates from time to time, because it gives you the opportunity to get to know them better while they get to know you. This doesn't mean you have to invite them to your house for dinner, but you might want to ask them out for coffee, drinks, or lunch. Getting to know someone outside the office allows you to relax a bit and connect on a whole new level.

2. *True*. More and more executives are playing golf today, so it is helpful to know a few simple rules, in case you find yourself on the links. Private country clubs have specific dress codes for men and women, which call for shorts or chinos, not jeans. When you are playing golf at a public course, you can wear whatever you please. Golfers at private clubs dine at either a grill, which is casual, or a formal dining room, so never ask for the "restaurant" if you are at a country club. Also, most country clubs do not deal in cash, except perhaps for caddy gratuities, so make sure to bring a credit card.

3. *True*. If you want to be at the top of your game in today's global business world, it's important to understand that different countries have different codes of behavior. Most Americans know, for example, that Asians do not shake hands, they bow. In Mexico it is customary for the *arriving* person to greet others first. In France, people greet their friends with two or more kisses on each cheek. In Russia, women often walk arm in arm with their female friends. Knowing and respecting customs and cultural differences will reflect well on you and make it easier to assimilate so you can conduct business. Ignoring cultural differences can blow a deal—or, at the very least, create some awkward moments.

4. *True*. You should carry your business cards with you wherever you go, even to the supermarket, because you never know whom you might meet. You might not always want to give it out, but you should never leave home without one.

5. *True*. Not giving out your business card unless you are asked is a little-known but important etiquette rule. This is especially true if you are with a senior-level person. The exception to this rule is at a business meeting or networking event, when it is expected that you exchange cards.

6. *True*. When networking, try to keep your right hand free, so you can shake hands with people you meet. If you are having cocktails, hold your drink in your left hand. Do not try juggling an hors d'oeuvres plate and a drink, because you won't be able to do both. Remember, you're not there to eat and drink; you're there to meet and greet!

7. *True*. Don't return to the buffet table more than once at a business function, because you would be wasting good time that you could devote to networking. Plus, you can't talk with your mouth full. Eat before you go, so you won't be hungry and tempted to graze.

8. *True*. It is bad form to abandon someone you have just met at a party. Introduce that person to someone else, and then excuse yourself before circulating.

9. *True*. It is OK, especially for Americans, to call a business peer by his or her first name. If someone is at a higher level, wait for an introduction to get an idea of how to address him or her.

10. *True*. It is a sign of respect to address an elderly person as Mr., Mrs., or Ms., unless he or she tells you otherwise. While this kind of formality is disappearing in the workplace, you might encounter people at a senior level who remember when this was the accepted form of address rather than the exception.

11. *True*. Always start your business introductions with the highest-ranking person first. As in the military, business follows a chain of command, and CEOs, like generals, outrank the privates or junior executives.

12. *False.* When you are at a lunch meeting, you want to ease into business so that you will have a chance to enjoy your food. Start with some small talk over appetizers before you move into the business entrées.

13. *False.* Breakfast meetings are by nature faster and less formal than lunches or dinners, so they are often reserved for getting to know a client or colleague. This doesn't mean you can't talk business, but you don't necessarily have to jump right in before your eggs and coffee.

14. *True.* Growing your circle of influence is a good way to stay up-to-date with what's going on in your industry and to make connections that you might need later on in your career, should you decide to change jobs or companies. Networking can be as varied as going out for coffee, playing a game of tennis with colleagues, and writing a few quick e-mails to catch up with other people in your industry.

15. *False.* Placing a video on YouTube can be helpful if you are in a creative field like entertainment or advertising, but most businesses do not look to YouTube as a place to find potential hires. Better places for online networking are the networking sites LinkedIn and Plaxo.

16. *False.* If your boss is a woman and you are a man, she should be the one picking up the check. You are not dating; you are having a business meal.

17. *False.* Never take a client to a restaurant you haven't been to before, even if you heard it was good. You wouldn't try out a

▶ ELEGANT SOCIAL SKILLS ▶▶▶

Your mother was right when she told you to mind your manners. Remembering the following basic protocols will give you what I consider elegant social skills:

- ▶ Smile and greet people you know when you pass them in the hallway or on the street.
- ▶ Say "please" and "thank you." (You would be surprised at how many people forget their basic manners.)
- ▶ Admit when you are wrong.
- ▶ Have a sense of humor.
- ▶ Remember people's names.
- ▶ Be sensitive to another person's point of view.
- ▶ Return phone calls and e-mails within twenty-four hours.

new recipe at a dinner party, so why run the risk of having a bad experience at a business meal? Plus, you often get better service at places where you are a regular customer.

The following social-protocol quiz will help you assess your business manners.

▶▶ ANSWER TRUE OR FALSE:

1. I order first when dining out, so my companion will feel more comfortable.
2. Beverages should always be served from the right, and food served from the left.
3. It is OK to have more than two alcoholic drinks at a business lunch.

4. I understand the difference between dining American and Continental style.
5. When eating a salad, it is OK to use a fork to cut the lettuce.
6. I pass food to the right.
7. I always season my food first before I taste it.
8. I tip only for good service.
9. I put my napkin on the table when I leave to go to the rest room.
10. I always ask the price of an item of food when ordering.
11. The bread-and-butter plate is on the right side of a place setting.
12. Complaining about the food shows that I have high standards.
13. It is not necessary to make reservations for lunch or breakfast.
14. I like to arrive "fashionably late" to a dinner party.
15. I always send a thank-you note after being taken out to a restaurant.
16. It's OK for me to talk or text on a cell phone when I'm in a restaurant.

Answers:

These answers will help you see what you might need to change about your social skills.

1. *False.* A good rule of thumb is to let the person being taken out to dinner order first. If you are going dutch, then "ladies first" should apply. If you're all women, let the person who is ready to order go first.

2. *True*. If you are throwing a dinner party, remember to serve the beverages from the right with your right hand, and serve the food from the left with your left hand. This is the way fine restaurants do it. You can make an exception if you don't have access to both sides of a guest.

3. *False*. While it's true that alcohol is a social lubricant, be careful not to have more than two drinks at a business lunch. Cocktails can loosen our tongues and inhibitions, and you do not want to say or do something you might regret later on.

4. *True*. The American style of dining means you place your knife down on your plate after cutting your food. The Continental style involves keeping your fork in your hand after cutting your food and eating with the fork facing down. Decide which method works best for you, and use it. Europeans also eat salads and cheese after their entrée. European portions tend to be smaller than Americans are used to, so don't complain to the waiter at a French restaurant that you were shorted. Eating reasonable portions is one reason why Europeans don't suffer as much from obesity as we super-size-loving Americans do.

5. *False*. If you don't need to cut your salad leaves, don't, but sometimes it is necessary, depending on the types of greens being served. If you are given a salad knife, use that. If not, it's probably best to use any available knife to make eating your salad more manageable, so it doesn't look like it's feeding time at the zoo.

6. *True*. Always pass your food to the right after serving yourself. The exception to this rule arises if the dish has already made the rounds in the other direction. In that case, you should go with the flow.

7. *False.* Always taste your food before you season, because you don't know whether or not the dish needs any more condiments until you try it.

8. *False.* Waiting tables is a tough job, and your servers might be having a bad day, so give them the benefit of the doubt, and tip. Waiters rely on tips for most of their earnings. How much you tip depends on the level of service you received. Tip 20 percent of the bill for excellent service and 15 percent for an efficient job—less only if you were ignored completely or treated rudely.

9. *False.* Always put your napkin on the chair when you go to the rest room. Putting your napkin on the table means you are leaving. In fine restaurants, the server will refold your napkin and place it back on the table while you're gone.

10. *False.* Do not ask the price of the food before ordering; that's what menus are for. You can ask to hear the specials if your server hasn't already given you a rundown the chef's selections. If the specials aren't listed on the menu, many servers will give the prices at that time. If not and you are concerned about price, go with something on the menu.

11. *False.* The bread-and-butter plate should always be on the left side of the place setting above the fork. The butter knife should be laid on the small plate diagonally. Water and wine glasses are on the right above the knife.

12. *False.* If you are someone's guest, do not complain about the food, no matter how bad you think it is. It will make you look like a whiner, not a gourmet. Should there be a legitimate problem with your food, discreetly tell the waiter, not the host, what the trouble is.

13. *False.* As you would do for dinner, it's a good idea to make reservations for breakfast and lunch, even if you think the restaurant won't be crowded. If you take your chances, you might not get a table, which is annoying and embarrassing if you are taking someone out. Plus, restaurants appreciate the notice.

14. *False.* The only thing you accomplish by being late for a dinner party is to make yourself look disrespectful. If the invitation says dinner at 8:00 P.M., coming a half hour later will throw off the host's schedule and keep other guests hungrily awaiting your arrival.

15. *True.* Always send a thank-you note after being taken out to a restaurant, whether it is handwritten or an e-mail.

16. *False.* It is rude to text or speak on a cell phone when you are at a restaurant, especially if you have dining companions. If you must be reachable in case of an emergency, put your phone on vibrate, and excuse yourself from the table to take the call. The same goes for cell phone use in elevators, on public transportation, at cinemas and theaters, or anywhere you have a captive audience.

Anna's Social-Image Tips

The following advice will help you to feel comfortable in almost any situation, whether you are at your office holiday party, having dinner with a friend, or on a business trip abroad.

A Party Where You Don't Know Anyone

We've all been there. You walk into a room where you don't know anyone, and everyone else is standing around in seemingly impenetrable clutches. What do you do? The first thing you need to do is to seek out someone who is standing alone. If you can't find anyone who is solo, try groups of three or more. Never break into a group of only two, because they might be having a private conversation. If the group is larger than five, you can get lost in the crowd, which is fine if you don't mind stepping back and observing for a while. I also recommend going to the host, who will introduce you to someone at the party. Offering to help the host is also a good idea. It is easier to break the ice when you are literally breaking some ice to hand someone a drink!

Faux Pas Fixes

Have you ever been at a party where you have forgotten the name of someone you've known for years? Have you ever spilled red wine on a dinner companion or a host's white rug? These common yet embarrassing social faux pas moments don't have to send you running for the exit. There are ways to gracefully get out of the most uncomfortable situations. Here are ten tips to take along with you to your next social event:

1. You have forgotten someone's name. Admit it. Do not pretend you know someone's name when you don't. Just say, "I'm so sorry, I've forgotten your name," or, "I remember great faces but not names; what is your name again?"

2. You have been introduced by the host, but he or she did not use your name. When the reverse happens, take pity and say your name when you shake hands with the person you are being introduced to: "Anna Wildermuth—nice to meet you." If you are in a crowd and the host has neglected to introduce you at all, make the move yourself. With someone you've met in the past, reintroduce yourself by saying, "I don't know if you remember me. I'm Anna Wildermuth."

3. You've spilled a drink on a dinner companion. Do not touch the person you've spilled your drink on. Instead, call the waiter or waitress over immediately. Offer to pay for the dry cleaning. If the person is a woman and she refuses, send flowers the next day. If it is man, send him a great business book. Apologize sincerely, and then let it go.

4. You freeze in the middle of a toast. Take a deep breath, pause to collect your thoughts, and pick up where you left off. You can also begin the sentence again, which might jog your memory. Make sure to look for a friendly face to help you relax. It can help to make a joke about it by saying something like, "Sorry, I'm having a senior moment," if applicable, or, "Sorry, I got so excited about what I was saying, I lost my place." My preference is to take a deep breath and start again to avoid a break in the momentum.

5. Someone has had too much to drink and starts heckling or being rude while you're making a toast. Stop your speech, and calmly turn to the host to ask that the offending person be removed. You can also politely ask the person to leave the room yourself, and do not start again until he or she leaves. Whatever you do, do not engage the rude person in an argument. Other than professional comedians, most people don't have the verbal artillery to deal with hecklers.

6. Someone has made an ethnic or sexist joke. Give this person a pass, especially if you suspect that he or she is unaware of how offensive the joke was. Ignore the joke without laughing, and quickly start another conversation. If the person has made an

---

▶ **YOU WON'T GET A SECOND CHANCE TO MAKE A GOOD FIRST IMPRESSION** ▶▶▶

In 2007, I conducted an unscientific survey of approximately 300 men and women who went to my Illinois workshops, asking them to identify the most important factor in arriving at first impressions. The participants included Caucasians, African-Americans, Latinos, and Asians between the ages of 20 and 60. As expected, clothes and face topped the list, but I was surprised (and secretly pleased) that age came in last. Here are the top ten things my students noticed about someone they had just met:

1. Clothing
2. Facial expression
3. Posture
4. Hair
5. Eye contact
6. Smile
7. Hygiene
8. Confidence
9. Speech
10. Age

offensive joke in a group, it's even easier to ignore it and move on, if those around you do the same.

7. You're talking to someone who is unbearably boring, and you want to circulate without hurting his or her feelings. This is called the breakaway. You say, "Let's go talk to [*another person in the room*]." You take the person to another group, stay awhile, and then tell the person you see someone in the room you have been trying to get a hold of for some time. Tell the boring person it was good to see him or her and hope you will see each other again before you leave.

8. Someone asks you how much you make. Tell the person you had a good year or that it was close to meeting your expectations, but don't give a figure. If you are self-employed, say, "I'll have to ask my accountant. He [or she] keeps track of my finances."

9. Someone starts gossiping about another person you both know. According to a University of Michigan study, when it comes to gossip, the most powerful person is the one who is receiving the information. You can put an end to gossip by not acknowledging it and changing the subject. Changing the subject sends the message that you are not interested in spreading the news.

10. You run into someone with whom you've had a falling-out. If the person says hello, you want to be courteous and return the greeting with a smile. It is your choice whether to make small talk or not. If you were the wronged party, a smile followed by a simple hello before moving on is sufficient. If the other person was the wronged party, you can make small talk to check out the reception and, after a bit of conversation, apologize again. If he or she is ignoring you, look for favorable body language and eye contact to help you make the decision about whether or not to approach.

Multicultural Business Etiquette

While it's hard enough to remember which fork to use when eating out, chances of making a faux pas are even greater when you're traveling abroad. If your company hasn't provided you with some cultural background information, go online (perhaps to a government-sponsored website) or buy a travel guide, and do your homework before you get off the plane. Here are some customs to keep in mind when doing business abroad:

- ▶ **China.** In China it is insulting to finish all the food on your plate and ask for seconds, because the host will think you were not given enough food. And don't discuss business over dinner when you first meet someone. Keep the conversation light until you get to know your host.
- ▶ **Eastern Europe.** Americans are accustomed to greeting one another with a cheery, "How are you?" and getting an equally sunny, "Fine, thanks. How are you?" in response. This kind of question is deemed odd, however, in Eastern Europe, where one is more likely to give a more honest answer, such as "Terrible!" Therefore, a simple "hello" will suffice.
- ▶ **Germany.** If you are celebrating a birthday in Germany, it is up to you as the birthday boy or girl to provide a treat for your well-wishers, not the other way around. Make sure

you take some goodies with you to work if your coworkers know it's your birthday.

▶ **Japan.** Ginsu knives aside, it's not a good idea to give a Japanese person knives as a gift, because it symbolizes cutting ties with the recipient.

▶ **Middle East.** People from Middle Eastern countries do not use their left hand for greetings or to hand an object to someone, because the left hand is considered unclean.

CAN YOU HEAR
ME NOW?

Change One Thing About Your
Communication Style

▶▶ THERE'S NO QUESTION that the ability to communicate with others effectively is an essential part of doing business. It involves being a good listener and knowing how to speak clearly and concisely. It means not speaking too fast or too slow. It means looking people directly in the eye when you are having a conversation, and not standing too close or being too standoffish.

Part of being a team player in business is being in sync with others, and you can do this by paying attention to the way you communicate. If you speak too fast, you run the risk of losing the other person's attention or respect. If you ramble on from one sentence to another, you will sound unfocused or flighty. Speaking too slowly will bore people or make them want to jump in to finish your sentences. Pay attention to your audience. If they look shell-shocked or confused, you've lost them.

Professor Alex Portland of the Massachusetts Institute of Technology recently invented a smart phone that allows users to evaluate their conversations for tone, cadence, and the number of times one interrupts. Dr. Portland believes people can someday use the data to change their unproductive speech patterns and improve workplace dynamics. Until then, you can assess your own speech patterns and tones by recording yourself or calling your voice mail and leaving a message. Listen for the speed and clarity of your voice. Are you high-pitched? Do you mumble or speak too softly? Whatever your particular problem is, ask a friend to give you a gentle nudge in the ribs whenever you fall off the wagon.

The following quiz will help you define and refine your communication style.

▶▶ ANSWER TRUE OR FALSE:

1. I always look people in the eye when talking or listening to them.
2. I keep an arm's length away from someone I'm talking to.
3. I am comfortable making small talk.
4. I am comfortable talking to people I do not know.
5. I am comfortable talking to people I do know.
6. I am comfortable speaking in front of a small group.
7. I am comfortable speaking in front of a large group.
8. Most people find me easy to talk to.
9. I can clearly explain what I do in under a minute.
10. I organize my thoughts before I speak.

11. I enunciate clearly.
12. I'm a good listener.
13. I ask questions.
14. When I first meet someone, I use his or her name at least once during our conversation.
15. I smile frequently.
16. I respect others' opinions, even if I disagree with them.
17. People can hear me when I speak.

Answers:

1. *True.* Always make eye contact when you are talking to someone. Eye contact shows confidence in yourself and says you are interested in what the other person is saying. People who have trouble making eye contact appear shifty, shy, or uncomfortable.

2. *True.* Most people maintain this distance naturally, but some cultures are closer talkers than others. Personal space is important in the United States, so always stay an arm's length away from the person you are talking to. Where do you think the expression "too close for comfort" came from?

3. *True.* People with good social skills are comfortable making small talk, no matter how inane the topics. If you have trouble with this, read newspapers and magazines (gossip magazines are good for conversation starters), watch the TV newscasts, or go online to check out some blogs. Seeing the latest movie or reading a good book is also helpful, but the other person has to have read or seen what you have to make this work, so you should always have something else in your small-talk arsenal just in case.

4. *True.* If you are uncomfortable meeting new people, practice by striking up conversations with strangers. The next time you are in a checkout line, ask the person in front of you about an item he or she is purchasing. For example, "Is that good? I've always wanted to try it." It doesn't matter what you say, as long as you practice meeting new people. Complimenting someone on an article of clothing or piece of jewelry is another good way to strike up a conversation: "I like your shoes; where did you get them?" Women have an easier time doing this than men, but most men use sports as their universal language.

5. *True.* If you are uncomfortable talking to people in general, make sure that you smile often and reflect back on what others are saying until you feel more relaxed and ready to speak up.

6. *True.* Speaking in front of a small group is a whole lot easier than speaking in front of a room full of people. If you responded False to this statement, join a book club, which usually has no more than ten people in a group, and talk about a book you've just read. Any club that doesn't have a large membership will work as well.

7. *True.* I frequently speak in front of large audiences, and sometimes I still get the jitters, so if this describes you, don't feel bad! I usually just say to myself, "Anna, get over it!" This may or may not work for you, but it does for me. If you are speaking in front of a large group, seek out a friendly face, and talk directly to that person. Look around the room for someone who is nodding or smiling. Keep in mind that unless you are a celebrity, people are not there to see *you*; they are there to get the information you are giving. Remembering this will take some of the pressure off.

8. *True*. One of the keys to being a good communicator is for other people to find it easy to talk to you. If they don't, you are probably coming off as intimidating. Watch your facial expressions and body language. Do you frown a lot? Do you fold your arms in front of you? Do you refuse to make idle chitchat? Find out what is putting other people off, and change it!

9. *True*. Make sure you know how to explain what you do in thirty to sixty seconds. Think of that explanation as a commercial for yourself! This is especially important when you are networking or during a job interview. How do you serve the public or company you work for? Even more important is communicating that you love what you do. Enthusiasm goes a long way.

10. *True*. I mention this a lot, but I can't emphasize it enough. Take time to organize your thoughts before you speak. When you are asked about a topic that requires some explanation, you could say, "That's a good question," which will give you a moment to pause and think before you speak.

11. *True*. A crucial part of being a good communicator is being understood. When you mumble, people are forced to ask you to repeat what you've just said, which is tiresome. Practice reading a paragraph with a pencil in your mouth. Then take the pencil out, and read the paragraph again. I know it sounds strange, but this trains the muscles to work harder when you speak.

12. *True*. Many people like to hear themselves speak, but conversation is a give-and-take. Make sure you listen. Being a good listener not only shows respect for others, it's also one of the most important qualities a businessperson can have, because the opinions of others will inform your own decisions.

13. *True.* One of the ways to show you are a good listener is to reflect on what the other person is saying. You can do this by asking questions. Don't assume; ask.

14. *True.* Using a person's name a few times during the course of a conversation will help you remember it in the future. It also helps you learn the correct pronunciation, should they have an unusual name.

15. *True.* Don't be fake or clownish, but smiling makes just about everyone look more attractive and approachable.

16. *True.* Never dismiss someone else's opinion, even if you disagree. Simply agree to disagree, and leave it at that.

17. *True.* Are you often asked to repeat yourself like that "Can you hear me now?" commercial for a cell phone company? If you are a low talker, practice projecting by standing in front of a friend and saying your name. Then, move an arm's length away, and continue saying your name so your friend can hear you. Put your hands on your throat so you can feel what it is like to speak up. (See the next section for more communication style tips.)

Your Voice Speaks Volumes About Your Personality

Even if you have a sterling résumé, looking good on paper is not always enough for you to get that promotion you've been vying for or to reach that next round of interviews in your job search.

The truth is, your voice speaks volumes about your personality, and it can have a negative or positive effect on your personal and professional life. A recent Stanford University study found that people make judgments about a person's credibility based on the way he or she speaks. Listen to a recording of yourself to figure out what your speaking style is, and then read the following tips for working on what needs fixing.

▶ **High-pitched talkers.** If you have a squeaky or high-pitched voice, people might think you are insecure and inexperienced. Grown women who sound like little girls are not always taken seriously by their coworkers. High-pitched talkers will be shunned because no one wants to be in the same room with someone who sounds like a smoke alarm.

Quick-fix change: Having a voice that naturally sounds like Minnie Mouse doesn't mean you have to stay that way forever. Invest in a session or two with a professional speech pathologist or vocal coach to see if you can take it down a notch or two.

▶ **Slow talkers.** Slow talkers can come across as confident and often gain the respect of their colleagues. If you talk slowly, you have a calming effect on others (think yoga teachers), because you appear to be relaxed and in control. If you speak *too* slowly, however (think Ben Stein as the teacher in *Ferris Bueller's Day Off*), with several seconds elapsing between words for no apparent reason, you will irritate others, who are silently begging you to get to the point already!

Quick-fix change: Try listening to someone who speaks at a normal clip, and practice mimicking their tempo while reading a book until you pick up the pace a bit. Drink a double espresso before doing this exercise, and see if that helps.

▶ **Nasal talkers.** Studies have shown that most people are annoyed by those who have a nasal quality to their voices and sound as if they have a perpetual cold. Nasal speakers come off as demanding and calculating, and therefore as less professional.

Quick-fix change: Look at yourself in the mirror to see if you are opening your mouth wide when you speak. If you aren't using the muscles in your mouth, practice by exaggerating the mouth movements a bit more as you talk, so the sound waves come from your voice box instead of from your nose.

▶ **Gravelly voice.** People who have gravelly voices give off an air of authority and experience. Gravelly talkers are often well liked by their coworkers, and singers often cultivate this sound in order to give their voices a more soulful, edgy quality.

Quick-fix change: I'm not suggesting you take up smoking cigarettes in order to sound like Lauren Bacall or Janis Joplin. In fact, if you find that your voice is getting increasingly gravelly, see your doctor to rule out some kind of health or throat problem. If you *are* a smoker, you know what you should do.

▶ **Fast talkers.** Fast talkers are sometimes thought to be nervous and flighty—not particularly good qualities to have attributed to you in the workplace.

Quick-fix change: As I mentioned earlier, pause between sentences by taking a deep breath before you speak. This will give you time to compose your thoughts and will allow your coworkers to jump in, should they want to get a word in edgewise.

▶ **Low talkers.** One of the funniest "Seinfeld" episodes was about a low talker who asked Jerry to wear one of the puffy shirts she designed for his appearance on the "Tonight Show." He unwittingly agreed because he couldn't hear what she was saying! You don't want people to have to work so hard to hear you, and low talkers come across as being meek or shy. Conversely, low talkers who have a deep, powerful tone to their voice (think Paul Robeson) can exude strength and confidence. In other words, you can speak softly if your voice carries a big stick. Otherwise, you'll want to work on it.

Quick-fix change: To make sure you are being heard when you speak, check for visual clues from the people you are talking to. If they are nodding their heads blankly, chances are they haven't heard a word you've said. To get a feel for what it sounds like to project, practice by speaking to a friend who is standing across the room. Do this until you feel comfortable with raising your voice. It's probably a good idea to avoid talking to older folks with hearing aids until you master this.

Sloppy Speech Habits

In addition to the tone of your voice, you must also pay attention to what you are saying. Even those with the most mellifluous speech can make someone cringe by being a sloppy speaker. Here are some common mistakes to look out for:

▶ **Hemming and hawing.** Fillers such as *um, ah, OK, you know,* and *like* are the brain's way of taking a nap. If you need to pause to get your thoughts together, it's better to say nothing at all than to hem and haw like a teenager.

▶ **Slang.** You don't always have to sound like a college professor, but using too much slang can be a verbal crutch. Once in a while is fine, but not so that every sentence is "your bad."

▶ **Bad grammar.** Bad grammar, like bad spelling, can make you appear, well, dumb, so bone up on your grammar by reading more and paying attention to those who speak well. Some common mistakes:

> **Incorrect:** "Me and my friend went to the store."
> **Correct:** "My friend and I went to the store."

> **Incorrect:** "There are a myriad of problems with this report."
> **Correct:** "There are myriad problems with this report."

> **Incorrect:** "There were less people at the event than I thought."
> **Correct:** "There were fewer people at the event than I thought."

> **Incorrect:** "So I says to him, 'Don't say that.'"
> **Correct:** "So I said to him, 'Don't say that.'"

> **Incorrect:** "I don't know nobody who is smarter than my boss."
> **Correct:** "I don't know anyone who is smarter than my boss."

> **Incorrect:** "It ain't just you who talks that way."
> **Correct:** "It isn't just you who talks that way."

▶ **Mispronouncing words.** Be careful not to say "axe" instead of "ask," "wif" instead of "with," "tree" instead of "three," "ath-a-lete" instead of "athlete," or "talkin'" instead of "talking." Speak clearly and say the entire word, including the gerund.

▶ **Clichés.** Lazy speakers often sprinkle their conversation with clichés when they can't come up with anything else. Avoid overusing clichés like "the whole nine yards," "at the end of the day," or "thinking outside the box."

▶ **Wimpy words.** Watch out for wimpy words like *kind of, sort of, maybe,* or *hopefully,* which weaken your message and make you seem less confident.

Words That Sell

At a recent workshop, I recorded a video of someone giving a presentation to sell an e-business service. Afterward, the presenter and I went back to watch his presentation, looking for words he used that sold us on his venture. Here are some examples of powerful words from his and other successful presentations:

- ▶ **You.** Ask your audience, "How do you feel about this? What are your needs?" Personalizing your product or service will help people understand how it directly affects them.
- ▶ **Cost-effective.** Most people in business are interested in the bottom line, which boils down to this question: How will this help us save or make money? Try to include the bottom line in all your pitches.
- ▶ **Benefit.** How does this service or product benefit the user, in addition to saving money or helping him or her make more? Does it make the person's life or business a bit easier?
- ▶ **Value.** What is the overall value of what you are selling? Can you attach a dollar figure (this painting is worth $1 million on the market), or is it impossible to quantify, making it "invaluable"?

▶ **Safety.** Is your product safe to use? Is there risk involved in trying it? Safety can be about either physical or financial risk.

▶ **Expectations.** What are your client's expectations? Make sure you communicate how you are going to meet these expectations.

▶ **Love.** It might be a soft word, but love packs a powerful punch. Adding the emotional element to what you are selling will make your pitch even stronger.

▶ **Easy.** No matter how good a product or service is, if it's too complicated to use, no one will go for it. Let your audience know that using what you are selling is a piece of cake.

▶ **Proven.** Do you have statistics, studies, or results to back up your claims? If so, make sure to trot those out.

▶ **Guarantee.** This is a very effective word, but don't say it unless you are prepared to put your money where your mouth is by offering a money-back guarantee if the customer isn't satisfied!

You might want to include some of these words the next time you are pitching a service, product, or yourself.

E-Mail Etiquette

With e-mail becoming the preferred form of communication in business today, it is important to know the proper e-mail etiquette, so you will convey the correct professional image and get your point across quickly and efficiently. Remember, e-mails leave a paperless trail and can easily go viral with one quick click of the mouse, so be careful what you send or post online. E-mail etiquette rules will differ according to the nature of your business and the corporate culture, but the following list offers guidelines that apply to nearly all companies:

▶ **Be concise and to the point.** Do not make an e-mail longer than it needs to be. Get to the point, and try not to ramble. E-mail should be a time-saver, not a time waster.

▶ **Answer all questions, and preempt further questions.** An e-mail reply should answer all questions to minimize follow-up. Sometimes people read e-mails too quickly and skip parts of the message. Try cutting and pasting the original message and responding below to each, so you don't miss anything.

▶ **Use proper spelling, grammar, and punctuation.** Using improper spelling, grammar, and punctuation makes a bad impression. It's a little like verbal slouching. Most computer systems have a spell-checker, so use it!

▶ **Make it personal.** If you are doing an e-mail blast to many different people, don't forget to personalize it by using the recipient's names. People tend to respond better when a message is addressed to them.

▶ **Use templates for frequently used responses.** While it's important to personalize your message by addressing each recipient by name, it is OK to use a template if you are doing an e-mail blast. Use your templates in a Word document, or use preformatted e-mails. Even better is a tool such as ReplyMate for Outlook (which allows you to use ten templates for free).

▶ **Answer swiftly.** You should respond to business e-mail within twenty-four hours, if possible. If the e-mail is complicated, just send an e-mail back saying that you have received it and will get back to the sender. Ignoring an e-mail is impolite and leaves the sender questioning whether or not the message was received.

▶ **Do not attach unnecessary files.** Sending large attachments is annoying and can clog up an e-mail system. Wherever possible, try to compress attachments and send attachments only when they are productive. Moreover, you need to have a good virus scanner in place, because downloading attachments can spread viruses.

▶ **Do not use crazy fonts or colors.** Unusual typefaces and colors are fine for personal e-mails, but your business e-mails should be in black and white.

▶ **Do not write in CAPITALS.** WRITING IN CAPITALS MAKES IT APPEAR AS IF YOU ARE SHOUTING. Not only is this format annoying and difficult to read, it might trigger a nasty response in the form of flame mail.

▶ **Don't leave out the message thread.** Remember to include the original mail along with your reply. Reading the original message will remind the recipient about the subject matter and put everything into context.

▶ **Read your e-mail before you press Send.** Read over your e-mail before you send it out in order to avoid embarrassing spelling and grammatical mistakes or unintended phrasing. It's worth a minute or two of your time if you save face in the long run.

▶ **Do not overuse Reply to All.** When you're replying to a message, avoid using Reply to All unless you really need your message to be seen by each person who received the original message. There's nothing more annoying than having to open and read a message that was intended for someone else.

▶ **Use abbreviations and emoticons sparingly.** In business e-mails, it is not appropriate to use abbreviations such as BTW (by the way) and LOL (laughing out loud). It's not professional, and the recipient might not be aware of what these abbreviations mean. The same goes for emoticons, such as the smiley :-). Would you draw a smiley face on a business letter?

▶ **Do not forward chain letters.** Most people find chain letters annoying, so do not send them on to others. Most of them are hoaxes, and they should be tossed along with the other spam.

▶ **Do not use e-mail to send personal information.** Never send personal messages using your work e-mail. Some companies actually monitor workers' e-mail correspondence to eliminate goofing off, so you run the risk of your boss reading your most private thoughts.

▶ **Use a meaningful subject.** Never leave a subject line blank in a business e-mail. Try to choose a simple phrase that will let the recipient know the content before he or she has to open up the message.

▶ **Avoid using *urgent* and *important* in your subject lines.** Do not use these types of words in an e-mail or subject line unless the topic is truly an urgent matter. Otherwise, you will be like the boy who e-mailed "wolf"—your truly urgent e-mails will not be taken as seriously.

▶ **Do not forward offensive material.** If you pass along offensive material, you are putting yourself and your company in jeopardy of a lawsuit. Delete such messages immediately, or contact your IT manager if you are receiving offensive spam.

▶ **Remember to include a signature.** When you don't include a signature at the end of your e-mail, the message will seem as though it is hastily written. It's a little like a weak handshake. You must seal the message with a strong signature that includes your name, title, work address, phone number, and website, if you have one.

Tips for Improving Your Writing Image

Whether it's for an e-mail, memo, fax, or that horse-and-buggy snail mail, knowing how to write well is a skill that can boost your career and help you stand out from the pack. Like any other skill, it takes practice, so here are some ideas for becoming a better wordsmith.

▶ **Read.** We all have busy lives, but the best way to improve your writing skills is to read books, newspapers, and magazines. I'm not talking about the *National Enquirer*, romance novels, or comic books, which are fine for fun but won't help you improve your prose. Here are some publications where you will find well-written, elegantly crafted prose:

▷ **Newspapers:** *New York Times, Wall Street Journal, Washington Post*
▷ **Magazines:** *New Yorker, Vanity Fair, Esquire, Business Week, The Atlantic, Sports Illustrated, Time, Newsweek*

▷ **Books:** Anything by James Joyce, Henry James, Emily Brontë, D. H. Lawrence, William Shakespeare, Leo Tolstoy, William Faulkner, Charles Dickens, F. Scott Fitzgerald, Franz Kafka, Mark Twain, John Updike, Flannery O'Connor, Philip Roth, Ralph Ellison, Larry McMurtry, David McCullough, or Martin Amis.

▷ **Websites:** *Slate, Salon, Politico, Huffington Post, Daily Beast*

▶ **Edit your writing.** It's easier to write longer than it is to write short, so once you've put down a draft, go back and edit. Take out any extraneous words or sentences, so what is left is clear and, best of all, concise.

▶ **Don't use too many big words.** Some people think good writing means using as many syllables as possible. Not so. Good business writing isn't about showmanship, so don't use a big word when a shorter one will suffice.

▶ **Avoid jargon.** Every industry has its jargon, which is OK to use once in a while, but overdoing it is lazy writing.

▶ **Organize your thoughts.** Think of your writing as being like your closet. If everything is thrown in without a system, you've got a big, ugly mess on your hands. If you are writing a long report, make an outline first, so your writing isn't all over the place but has a beginning, middle, and end that make sense.

▶ **Don't bury your lead.** One of the rules of journalism is to lead off with the most important news. Don't waste your readers' time with long introductions that dance around the point you are trying to make.

▸ WORDS TO USE AND WORDS TO AVOID ▶▶▶

The following words and phrases are some of my favorites:

analysis	learn
answer	listen
brainstorm	manage
collaborate	offer
collaborative	open mind
confer	productive
control	profitable
cooperate	reduce
cost-effective	smart
effective	solve
emerge	successful
evaluate	synergy
expedite	team
experience	team player
good listener	team up
guide	thanks
hear	together
helpful	valuable
huddle	value
idea	vigorous
improve	work together
increase	

The following words and phrases are not a part of my regular business vocabulary:

afraid	can't
bad luck	cheated
blame	crisis

delay	insist
demand	loss
excuse	must
fail	nonnegotiable
fault	one-time offer
fear	overloaded
forgot	should
frustrating	sorry
guess	tired
impossible	unaware
impractical	unfair
inadequate	unreasonable

How to Handle Complaints

It's the rare job where you don't hear or deal with complaints, whether from coworkers, clients, or the public. Here are some tips for handling complaints gracefully and with the minimum of drama:

▶ Be empathetic and show your interest in the problem.
▶ Find areas of agreement, and express it.
▶ Remain kind and courteous, and try not to argue.
▶ Do not interrupt. Let the person vent.
▶ Do not pass the blame onto others.
▶ Explain clearly and calmly your suggestion for solving the problem.
▶ If you are at an impasse, offer to speak to your manager or someone else in your department.

▶ If you are at fault, apologize. Say, "I'm sorry" rather than "We're sorry," because it is more sincere.
▶ Act immediately to solve the problem. Don't let time pass.
▶ Follow up. Get back to the complainant to make sure the problem was solved to his or her satisfaction.

Communication Exercise 1: Conversation Tools

I got the idea for the following exercise after reading a book called *Crucial Conversations: Tools for Talking When Stakes Are High* by Kerry Patterson, Glenn Joseph, Ron McMillan, and Al Switzler (New York: McGraw-Hill, 2002). It should be done with a partner. Select a topic of conversation to discuss, preferably one that is controversial so that you can have an interesting exchange of ideas. After your conversation is finished, take turns answering the following questions. Discuss ways in which you can both improve your communication style based on the answers.

What did you notice about your partner's communication style?

Answer True or False:

▶ Avoided the main issue.
▶ Used jokes, sarcasm, or nasty remarks to hide frustration.
▶ Tried to change the subject.
▶ Used hyperbole to bolster arguments.
▶ Held back rather than give opinions.
▶ Interrupted often and seemed impatient.

▶ Tried to be nice to soften discussion.
▶ Acted defensively when challenged.
▶ Did not listen to the other person's opinion.
▶ Used body language to express frustration with the other person's opinion.
▶ Used facts to bolster points.
▶ Clearly and calmly expressed disagreement.

Where did your partner's communication style succeed or fail?

List three elements that succeeded in your conversation.

1. _____
2. _____
3. _____

List three elements that failed during the conversation.

1. _____
2. _____
3. _____

Answer the following questions about how you think your conversation went, and have your partner do the same.

▶ Did you experience a free flow of ideas?
▶ Did you communicate what you really wanted to say?
▶ How much emotional content was in your discussion?
▶ What was the underlying emotion?
▶ Did you stray from the issue?
▶ Did you want to win an argument or make a point at all costs?

▶ Did your conversation come from your head or from your heart?

▶ Did you get angry or frustrated with your partner?

▶ Did you respect your partner's opinions?

▶ Did you have a sense of humor?

Communication Exercise 2: First Impressions

The following exercise will reveal what kind of impression you make during conversations with people you've just met. This exercise should be done with a partner or in a group of no more than six people. Do not do this with friends. Introduce yourself, and talk casually for about fifteen minutes before taking turns filling out the following questionnaire. Make sure to use constructive criticism that is inclusive ("You might want to try smiling more," rather than "You seemed like the kind of person who would sell your grandmother for a promotion").

I find this person to be an authority figure (e.g., formal, powerful, intimidating).

Explain: _____

_____

I find this person to be approachable (e.g., friendly, fun-loving, easy going).

Explain: _____

_____

Describe this person's:

Facial expression (e.g., smiles, makes eye contact, nods) ————

————————————————————————————————

————————————————————————————————

Eyewear (e.g., color, shape, or style) ————————————

————————————————————————————————

————————————————————————————————

Color and clothing choices ————————————————

————————————————————————————————

————————————————————————————————

Body language ————————————————————

————————————————————————————————

————————————————————————————————

Voice tone (nasal, pitch) ————————————————

————————————————————————————————

————————————————————————————————

Voice projection (loud or soft) ————————————

————————————————————————————————

————————————————————————————————

Recommendations ————————————————————

————————————————————————————————

————————————————————————————————

————————————————————————————————

————————————————————————————————

Answer the following about yourself:

I want to look _____

_____

_____

Communication Exercise 3: Speech Profile

This exercise can be used after a conversation or presentation. Hand out a copy of the following questionnaire to your partner or audience. Ask listeners to circle the answers on the following scales. For each pair of words, 1 is the most negative rating, and 9 is the most positive.

Loudness or Volume

Too quiet	1	2	3	4	5	6	7	8	9	Easily heard
Inaudible	1	2	3	4	5	6	7	8	9	Easily heard
Flat	1	2	3	4	5	6	7	8	9	Vibrant

Pitch

High	1	2	3	4	5	6	7	8	9	Low
Shrill	1	2	3	4	5	6	7	8	9	Full
Monotonous	1	2	3	4	5	6	7	8	9	Varied

Voice Quality

Nasal	1	2	3	4	5	6	7	8	9	Open
Breathy	1	2	3	4	5	6	7	8	9	Clear
Harsh, raspy	1	2	3	4	5	6	7	8	9	Mellow
Lifeless	1	2	3	4	5	6	7	8	9	Enthusiastic

Articulation

Slushy	1	2	3	4	5	6	7	8	9	Clear
Lazy lips	1	2	3	4	5	6	7	8	9	Crisp
Tangled tongue	1	2	3	4	5	6	7	8	9	Controlled
Tight jaw	1	2	3	4	5	6	7	8	9	Open mouth
Mumbling	1	2	3	4	5	6	7	8	9	Projection
Mispronounced	1	2	3	4	5	6	7	8	9	Pronounced

Timing or Rate

Jerky	1	2	3	4	5	6	7	8	9	Smooth
Slow, prodding	1	2	3	4	5	6	7	8	9	Fluent
Unvaried	1	2	3	4	5	6	7	8	9	Varied, exciting
Hesitant	1	2	3	4	5	6	7	8	9	Deliberate

Vocal Variety

Emotionless	1	2	3	4	5	6	7	8	9	Emotional
Unfriendly	1	2	3	4	5	6	7	8	9	Genial
Strained	1	2	3	4	5	6	7	8	9	Natural
Dull	1	2	3	4	5	6	7	8	9	Vital

Source: Form provided by Toastmasters International.

Speaker Evaluation

After giving a speech or presentation, pass out this sheet to members of the audience, and ask them to fill it out so you can gain a better idea of what you need to change or strengthen as a public speaker. Use only one rating per category, and comments should explain the reason for the rating as well as suggestions for getting a higher score, if applicable.

Score Key: **5** = excellent
                     4 = very good
                     3 = acceptable
                     2 = marginal
                     1 = poor

Posture: Erect? Faced audience properly? Nervous? Slouched? Shifted weight?

Score: _____ **Comments:** _____

_____

_____

Eye contact: Balanced contact with everyone in room?

Score: _____ **Comments:** _____

_____

_____

Hand gestures: Confident and appropriate use of hands? Fidgety and nervous?

Score: _____ **Comments:** _____

_____

_____

Vocal: Proper volume? Good use of inflection? Good vocal connection with audience? Monotone? Boring?

Score: _____ **Comments:** _____

_____

_____

Energy: Positive and enthusiastic? Smile? Low energy and little enthusiasm? Too hyper?

Score: _____ **Comments:** _____

_____

_____

Clarity of description: Clear description of item? Unclear? Rambling?

Score: _____ Comments: _____

_____

_____

Clarity of persuasion: Clear reasons for presenter's position? Hard to follow?

Score: _____ Comments: _____

_____

_____

Handling of questions: Understood question and responded appropriately? Clear, logical answer? Good composure? Rambling and unfocused?

Score: _____ Comments: _____

_____

_____

Overall impact: Positive, confident, persuasive, engaging? Tepid, unsure, unconvincing, off-putting?

Score: _____ Comments: _____

_____

_____

Additional comments: _____

_____

_____

_____

_____

_____

_____

_____

Workplace Communication Exercise

The following test will help you gauge how effective you are as a communicator in the workplace. You might be able to guess the "right" answer, but this is not the point of the test. Try to answer honestly, even if you feel that your response is the not best one possible. Remember, this is for self-evaluation purposes only.

▶▶ **ANSWER TRUE OR FALSE:**

1. I communicate effectively.
2. People really listen to me.
3. People enjoy talking to me.
4. People believe what I say.
5. People value my opinion.
6. I speak with confidence.
7. I feel good when I speak.
8. I have no trouble saying what I mean.
9. I am persuasive.
10. I have a good vocabulary.
11. I am a good negotiator.
12. I usually get a fair deal.
13. I enjoy friendly "haggling."
14. I don't take arguments personally.
15. I don't raise my voice.

Scores:

Give yourself a point for every True answer. To rate your communication effectiveness, compare your total with the following scores:

13–15 = You are an outstanding communicator.

10–12 = You have great communication skills.

7–9 = You have very good communication skills.

5–6 = You have fairly good communication skills.

less than 5 = You need to work more on your communication skills.

7

YOUR MOST
IMPORTANT CRITIC

Change One Thing About
Your Self-Image

▶▶ EVER WONDER WHY some people walk into a room as if
they own it? Certain people attract others like magnets, not just
because of how they look, but because they have that little extra
confidence and charisma that makes the difference between
standing out and blending in with the crowd. For these people,
being successful in their professional and personal lives comes
naturally, but for others, it must be learned.

The following quiz will help you determine what you need
to change about the way you view yourself, so you can be one of
those people who enter a room feeling like a rock star!

▶▶ ANSWER TRUE OR FALSE:

1. I like myself most of the time.
2. I blame myself when things go wrong.
3. People frequently comment on how good I look.
4. I compliment others when I think they deserve it.
5. I hate it when people tease me, even if they are close friends.
6. I have high energy most of the time.
7. I smile frequently.
8. I don't like doing things that I'm not good at.
9. I'm afraid people won't like me when I meet them.
10. I am an optimist.
11. I can discuss my achievements easily.
12. I get angry when someone disagrees with me.
13. I have no problem admitting when I make a mistake.
14. I look people in the eye when I speak.
15. I have a firm handshake.
16. I enjoy making small talk.
17. I bite my lip when I get nervous.
18. I fiddle with my hair a lot.
19. I often rub the back of my neck when I'm nervous.
20. I fold my arms across my chest when I speak.
21. I gesture with clenched fists.

Answers:

1. *True.* If you like yourself most of the time, you have a healthy dose of self-esteem. If you answered False, you probably think everything you do is a monumental disaster. Having poor self-esteem will be apparent to others, so get some help by way of a good therapist, and work on improving your self-image every day. Being happy in your own skin is the foundation for everything else that you will do in life.

2. *False.* One of the major signs of poor self-esteem is the tendency to blame oneself whenever things go wrong. Everyone makes mistakes, but people who feel good about themselves are confident enough to know that they are not at the root of evil.

3. *True.* Whether it's the way they dress, their hair, or simply their attitude, people who are complimented often on they way they look are not necessarily the most beautiful people, but are those who radiate a positive self-image. If you can't remember the last time someone said, "You look maaah-velous," it's time for a change.

4. *True.* If you are the type of person who gives compliments freely when you feel they are deserved, you feel secure. People who withhold compliments are afraid another person's success only serves to show them up.

5. *False.* People who are capable of laughing at themselves and being self-deprecating have the strongest self-image. I'm not talking about the nasty teasing that is meant to hurt or humiliate, but the good-natured kind that friends often do with their close pals. If you are offended when someone jokes about an amusing personality trait or even a physical characteristic like your flaming red hair, you probably need to take steps to boost your self-esteem.

6. *True.* Unless one has an illness, sleeping a lot or feeling tired all the time can be a sign of depression. People with a high energy level tend to be confident and self-possessed, so if you are a low-energy person, you might want to examine the causes.

7. *True.* Once again, people who smile often (if genuine) are pleased with themselves and their lives in general. If you are a sourpuss, you can bet your face is reflecting the turmoil that is going on inside.

8. *False*. People who are not confident about themselves generally do not like taking the risk of trying something new. Because they're afraid of looking foolish or embarrassing themselves, they would rather stick to doing things they know they do well.

9. *False*. If you are afraid of meeting new people because you think they won't like you, you must not like yourself very much.

10. *True*. Not only are optimists happier with their lives, but studies have shown that they tend to be healthier as well. If you describe yourself as a pessimist, you probably think the world is conspiring against you. People who see the glass half full are more likely to look at the best in themselves and others.

11. *True*. We have been taught since childhood not to boast, but being able to discuss your achievements is essential in business. You don't have to brag like Donald Trump (although it seems to have worked for him), but it's OK to be proud of your accomplishments and to humbly let people know about them, especially when interviewing and networking.

12. *False*. When you take differences in opinion personally, you are showing a lack of confidence in yourself. People who are sure of themselves respect others' ideas and can agree to disagree without being angry or resentful.

13. *True*. Nobody's perfect, so if you can't admit to making a mistake, you are showing how insecure you really are. People who have a strong self-image are able to say, "I'm sorry; my mistake," because they know that the world doesn't end when we make an error.

14. *True.* One of the biggest signs of a poor self-image is avoiding eye contact. It's the body's way of saying, "I'm not worthy of this conversation!"

15. *True.* Your handshake is your calling card, so a limp grip means you don't feel confident enough to make a strong connection with others. Most men know this already, but women shouldn't be afraid of having a firm (not bone-crushing) handshake, especially with male colleagues. (See "What Your Handshake Says About You," later in this chapter.)

16. *True.* The ability to make small talk is one of the most important socializing tools, so those who are able to chitchat about seemingly frivolous topics are usually at ease with themselves and with others.

17. *False.* Biting your lip when you speak shows a lack of confidence about what you are saying. It also makes you appear less trustworthy.

18. *False.* Touching your hair, like biting your lip or blinking too much, is a nervous tic, and it's distracting to the listener. Women who twirl or flip their hair appear flirtatious or ditzy.

19. *False.* Rubbing the back of your neck shows that you are jittery or tired. People want to talk to those who have passion and energy, not those who look like they'd rather be napping.

20. *False.* Folding your arms is a classic defensive posture. If you do this when you are speaking, you are unconsciously showing others that they should step back.

21. *False.* If you find yourself unconsciously clenching your fists, you are feeling angry or vulnerable. Either way, you are ready for a fight.

The 10 Percent Rule

I learned about the 10 percent rule when I was a real estate agent. It was said that agents lose a certain percentage of sales, no matter how good they are, simply due to the law of averages. Likewise, they will probably get a percentage of sales for the same reason. I decided that this rule could also apply to one's personal life. I believe 10 percent of the people you meet are not going to like you for myriad reasons having nothing to do with you. Perhaps you or your name reminds them of someone they've known in the past and didn't get along with. Conversely, 10 percent of the people you meet are going to bond with you immediately because they relate to the way you look, your background, your job, or your personality. If you take this as a given, then I advise you not to waste your time with the 10 percent you can't win over and to concentrate on the ones who like you.

Years ago, I was married to a high-profile businessman. When I tried to befriend the people in his social circle, they snubbed me. I tried everything I could think of to get them to like me. I felt hurt and took their rejection personally. It wasn't until my husband asked me to invite them to a party at our house that I noticed these snooty people treated others the same way they treated me. I realized then that it was they, not I, who had a problem, and that I was wasting my time trying to connect with them.

As soon as I applied the 10 percent rule, I began to feel better about myself, because being with folks you truly bond with will bring out the best in you. Good energy helps you blossom. This rule of empowerment will help you write off those people who are not worth your time or effort, which would be better spent on the other 10 percent who want to be with you. When you feel confident about yourself, chances are that even more people will want to get to know you better.

So the next time you meet someone new, try to figure out which group he or she belongs to, so you don't jump through hoops trying to win someone over. Did you ever get that uncomfortable feeling when a comedian bombs because he or she is trying too hard to entertain the audience? It's the same thing in the social world. When you are with people who like you, the relationship has a natural flow. When you are networking for business, you want to be able to move smoothly from person to person. If there isn't any chemistry, move on, because that contact will be unlikely to help you anyway. You can usually tell within the first five minutes if the chemistry is there and that person is worth pursuing.

What Your Handshake Says About You

Handshakes are used in greetings and as a way to seal a deal, express thanks, let bygones be bygones, or say good-bye. The

way you shake says a lot about how you feel about yourself and
your ability to bond with others. Here's what a handshake reveals
about you:

▶ **The bone crusher.** Breaking bones or making people
wince when you shake hands is a sign of insecurity, because
you are overcompensating by trying to one-up the person
you are shaking hands with. You don't have to add so much
weight to your barbells in order to appear strong.

▶ **The limp fish.** Failing to fully grasp a person's hand also
is a sign of insecurity and fear. You are afraid of letting the
other person know you exist. Instead, be firm and make eye
contact while you shake.

▶ **The finger hook.** If you reach for someone's fingers instead
of the person's palm, you are conveying that you are on the
fence. Don't be so indecisive—go for it, and make a full
grab!

▶ **The clammy hand.** If your hands are cold and clammy,
shaking with you can be off-putting because you are showing your nerves. To make sure your hands are dry and
warm, rub them together vigorously (in private) before you
shake.

▶ **The two-handed grip.** The two-handed grip is a sign of
friendship and informality. Men need to be careful about
using this shake with women, lest they appear too familiar.

▶ **Not letting go.** If you hang on for dear life once you have
made contact, you are displaying your fears of abandon-
ment. Shake a few times, and then break.

▶ **Too many rings.** Be careful not to wear too many large
rings when you are shaking hands (not good business
attire anyway), because you will inflict physical pain on the
recipient when metal meets flesh.

▶ **Fist bump.** Save it for outside the office or for when you've just closed a deal or hit a home run for the company's baseball team. The same goes for the high-five.

▶ **The perfect shake.** The best handshake involves standing up as the person approaches or extending your hand when you are about three feet away. Angle your arm across your chest with thumb side up and make eye contact. Pump firmly two or three times before letting go.

Tips for Boosting Your Self-Esteem

It's not easy to change the negative messages that we tell ourselves, and it sometimes requires the help of a professional therapist. But there are some things you can do to help boost your self-esteem. This is not a one-shot deal. If you want to affect some real, permanent change in your life, you must do these things on a regular basis, which can range from once a day to ten times a day—however long it takes to change your negative self-perception.

▶ **Keep a success journal.** One regular practice I suggest to clients who need a boost of self-confidence is keeping a record of all the things they have accomplished on any given day. These success journals can contain a range of accomplishments, from the routine ("I helped my son with his homework today") to the impressive ("I spotted an error at work, and fixing it saved the company thousands of dollars"). Small, seemingly insignificant successes are just as important as major ones, and we often forget to give ourselves due credit. So write it all down, and read the journal before you go to bed or once a week to remind yourself of all your triumphs, large and small. You should also refer to your success journal before a job interview or networking event.

▶ **Affirmations.** I realize this word conjures up images of Al Franken's character Stuart Smalley lisping platitudes into a mirror. That said, it is sometimes helpful to repeat positive messages in order to push out all the negative ones that creep into our consciousness on a daily basis. In addition to reading and rereading your success journal, keep a card with an affirmative statement written on it nearby, so you can refer to it whenever you're feeling low. Messages like "People love talking to me" can be helpful before you go to a social event, for example.

▶ **Associate with positive, supportive people.** Are you surrounded by people who put you down or make you feel less worthy? Examine your friends and family members to see what messages they are sending you. If those messages are demeaning in any way, cut your ties, and find new, supportive friends. It might be hard in the beginning, but it will be well worth it in the long run.

▶ **Volunteer to help someone less fortunate than you.** One of the best ways to raise your self-esteem is to do something nice for someone else. Helping others who are less fortunate than you are (and believe me, no matter how bad you might feel, there is probably someone out there who feels worse) is good for boosting your self-esteem. Not only will you feel better about yourself, you might even feel better about the world in general.

▶ **Just say no.** People who have a low self-image are often afraid to say no to something they really don't want to do, when asked to do something at work or in their personal life. Learning how to say no is one of the most liberating and empowering things you can do and shows that you value your own time.

▶ **Treat yourself to something special.** If you've been denying yourself something special because you don't think you're worth it, go out and get or do it right now! See how great it feels to be good to yourself.

▶ **Gather a "kitchen cabinet."** Enlist a group of people you trust to be your personal "kitchen cabinet." Call on these friends or relatives to give you candid advice and feedback whenever you have a problem or are feeling low. Everyone needs advisers, so it's helpful to have a personal support group you can count on when you need a morale boost.

▶ **Be assertive.** It might go against your nature, but make an effort to speak up for yourself the next time you want to say something but are afraid to do so. The simple act of asserting yourself will be rewarding enough that doing it will be even easier the next time around.

Negative Thoughts: If You Think You're Going to Lose, You Will

Norman Vincent Peale (author of *The Power of Positive Thinking*), motivational speaker Tony Robbins, and Stephen Covey (author of *The 7 Habits of Highly Successful People*) all built their careers around the idea of thinking positively and visualizing yourself as a winner. Even the bestselling book *The Secret* is about how imagining your goals will help make them happen. Successful athletes, in any sport, must have a can-do, no-fail attitude in order to compete and ultimately win. It sounds trite, but it really, truly works.

If you are a pessimist by nature, figure out what triggers your negative feelings and thoughts. Is it speaking in public? Going to parties? Job interviews? Exams? When faced with a task that makes you jittery, don't tell yourself, "I'm so bad at this," or, "I'll never learn how to do this well." Acknowledge the problem by saying, "I know speaking in public isn't one of my strengths. I'm not going to be the best speaker, but I'm not going to be the worst." That's better than telling yourself you are going to fail.

Replace the negative thought with a positive one. Take all the negative words out of your vocabulary. If a negative thought pops into your head, get rid of it. Some people like to imagine that a bird or butterfly is carrying that word out of the top of their head. Choose your own image. I recently read a headline in *Inc.* magazine that said, "Think Rich!" Of course, just thinking about being rich won't make you wealthy if you are not also actively involved in attaining your goal, but your mind can motivate you into action.

Negative messages are like arrows that go right to the heart of our self-image. Giving yourself negative messages, which so many people do without even realizing it, will sabotage your chances of being successful in your career or life in general. Review the following list of some common negative thoughts. If some of these statements sound familiar, change the message by replacing it with one of the affirmations in the next section. Even if you don't believe the affirmation, say it to yourself, so there will be no room in your head for negativity.

▶ Most people around me are better off than I am.

▶ People won't like the real me.

▶ I'm afraid my friends will reject me if I speak my mind.

▶ I was a born loser.

▶ If I disappeared tomorrow, nobody would notice.

▶ I don't contribute anything of worth to society.

▶ I'll never amount to anything.

▶ Everything I touch turns into a disaster.

▶ I don't have any real friends.

▶ You can't trust most people.

▶ Everyone is out to get me.

Affirmations

If you've never used affirmations before, this practice might seem awkward at first, but give the following "I am" statements a try. Repeat those affirmations that work for you every day until you believe that what you are saying is true. Feel free, of course, to add your own:

▶ I am competent.

▶ I am energetic.

▶ I am strong.

▶ I am enthusiastic.

▶ I am intelligent.

▶ I am relaxed.

▶ I am beautiful.

▶ I am joyful.

▶ I am a good person.

▶ I am trusting.

▶ I am caring.
▶ I am generous.
▶ I am loving.
▶ I am courageous.
▶ I am smart.
▶ I am forgiving.
▶ I am creative.
▶ I am open.
▶ I am talented.

Also repeat the following "I can" statements that apply to you out loud or to yourself. Reminding yourself of your goals will help you grow or change something about yourself that you don't like.

▶ I can lose weight.
▶ I can stop smoking.
▶ I can heal.
▶ I can let go of guilt.
▶ I can gain self-confidence.
▶ I can let go of fear.
▶ I can take risks.
▶ I can change.
▶ I can be a winner.
▶ I can be positive.
▶ I can be strong.
▶ I can be a problem solver.
▶ I can handle my own problems.
▶ I can laugh and have fun.
▶ I can be honest about my feelings.
▶ I can be assertive.

▶ I can control my temper.

▶ I can succeed.

The following "I will" affirmations are more action oriented and can be substituted for the "I can" statements. Each of these affirmations is a positive statement about what you want to happen on any particular day.

▶ I will smoke less today.

▶ I will control my temper today.

▶ I will feel relaxed at the meeting.

▶ I will grow emotionally stronger each day.

▶ I will smile more at my coworkers today.

▶ I will acknowledge good things about me today.

▶ I will sleep easily tonight.

▶ I will face my fears courageously today.

▶ I will take on only what I can handle today.

▶ I will take care of my needs today.

▶ I will challenge myself to change today.

▶ I will manage my time better today.

▶ I will handle my finances wisely today.

▶ I will take a risk and grow today.

Visualizations

A study conducted several years ago by researchers at the University of Chicago showed the power that visualizations had on basketball players. The players were randomly placed into three groups. First, they were all tested for their free-throw proficiency. Next, group 1 went to the gym every day to practice free throws for an hour. The second group also went to the gym, but instead

of practicing, these players lay down and simply visualized themselves making successful shots. The third group did nothing at
all. At the end of a month, the three groups were tested again to
determine their free-throw skills.

The players who hadn't practiced at all showed no improve-
ment, and many in that group actually exhibited a drop in performance. Those who had physically practiced one hour each
day showed a performance increase of 24 percent. The amazing
part of this study is that the group of players who simply imagined themselves shooting hoops successfully improved nearly as
much, at 23 percent. The point is, for you to succeed at whatever
you do, you must tell yourself there is nothing you can't overcome. Injuries, fatigue, downturns, whatever the obstacle—you
must believe that you will win in spite of everything.

Experts have found that visualizing yourself doing something you are afraid of also can help calm yours fears. For example, before a presentation, imagine yourself speaking in front
of a group that is responding favorably to what you are saying.
If you are worried about asking your boss for a raise, imagine
yourself making a case for a pay increase where the outcome is
positive.

You can also, as a form of meditation, visualize a place, person, or pet that makes you feel more relaxed. In many cultures,
meditation is a common practice that improves one's emotional
as well as physical health. It should always be done in a quiet,
private spot where there are no distractions such as telephones,
computers, TVs, children, or anything that will interrupt your
moment of Zen.

Suggestions for Visualizations
▶ A vacation spot
▶ A room where you feel safe and comfortable

▶ A rainbow
▶ A loved one, such a spouse, partner, or child
▶ A dramatic sunset
▶ The ocean waves
▶ A snow-topped mountain
▶ Insert your favorite image here!

8

GET THE JOB THAT WORKS FOR YOU

Change One Thing About
Your Interview Style

▶▶ WHETHER YOU ARE looking for a job or simply "looking around" for what's out there, doing well on interviews is one of the most important skills to master. It gives an employer the chance to assess whether you are the right candidate for the position, and equally important, it gives you the opportunity to learn more about the job to see if it would be a good fit. It all comes down to preparation, practice, performance, and post-interview follow up.

I realize that going on interviews is anxiety producing for most people, but try to look at it as a learning experience. Remember that you are not on trial! Interviewers don't want to trip you up or humiliate you; they simply want to get to know you. You are actually doing employers a favor by taking the time to speak to them, because there is presumably a need for someone to fill a new position or a replace someone who has left. Try to relax and enjoy this time to shine!

What Is Your Interview Style?

There's no question that people who ace their interviews are aware of their strengths and weaknesses, comfortable talking about their successes, and able to project confidence when asked about their qualifications and expertise in their chosen field. Like individuals' fingerprints, people's interview styles are unique. Answer the following questions to determine what your interview style is, and work on the areas that need changing to improve your chances of landing that job. Remember, interviewing is a whole lot easier when your style matches that of your potential employers.

▶▶ ANSWER EACH QUESTION:

1. Do you feel excited or reticent when asked to be interviewed?
2. Do you prefer to speak in front of one person or several?
3. Are you a high-energy or low-key person?
4. Do you depend on a well-planned script, or are you spontaneous in your answers?
5. Do you work from a list of your successes, or can you list them from memory?

6. Is your manner of speaking slow and deliberate or fast and flowing?
7. What style of dress do you prefer, informal or formal?
8. Do you research the company before your interview by looking for information on the Internet?
9. Before your interview, do you visit the company and watch employees enter and leave the building to get a feel for the corporate culture?

Answers:

These answers will reveal what you need to change about your interviewing style.

1. *Excited*. People who do well in interviews look at them as golden opportunities for the employer to get to know how great they are. If you dread going on interviews, you should work on changing your attitude.

2. *Several*. The more people you can speak in front of, the better. Interviews are not always one-on-one, and you might be asked to meet several people on the team. If this is a problem for you, practice speaking in a group.

3. *High-energy*. Having high energy (if it's not over the top) usually goes over well in interviews, because it shows you are excited about the opportunity to interview and the possibility of working with the company. If you are a low-energy person, you might want to stick to jobs that involve research or numbers and have less social interaction.

4. *Both.* You should have some type of prepared answers for questions you know in advance are likely to be asked. You also must also be able to answer questions spontaneously to show that you can think on your feet.

5. *You can recite your successes from memory.* Keep a list of your successes handy as preparation and for psyching yourself up before the interview. Also, commit your top three success stories to memory, so you can tell them during the interview.

6. *Both.* Your speech pattern should be well paced, which means not too fast and not too slow. Pay attention to how your interviewer is speaking, and try to match his or her style.

7. *Depends.* Be careful to match your style of dress to that of your interviewer, industry, and region. If you prefer to dress formally, you will probably feel more comfortable in conservative industries like finance. Wearing a suit to a tech interview will make you feel like an odd duck when casual geek is the preferred mode of dress. At many companies, however, it is expected that you will wear a suit to an interview, even if you would not wear one daily in the job you're seeking, as a sign that you take the interview process seriously. So it's better to err on the side of too formal than too casual!

8. *Yes.* Always do your research before your interview by going to the company website and searching the Internet for the latest news about the company and its industry.

9. *Yes.* Visiting the company beforehand will give you a feel for the corporate culture and atmosphere, including what employees are wearing to work. If everyone is in T-shirts, I'm not suggesting you dress the same way for the interview, but you could wear a blazer instead of a suit.

Types of Interviews

During a job search, you might encounter several different types of interviews, and you need to adjust how you prepare for each.

Information interviews are meetings you schedule for research purposes only. These are often the best kind of interviews to go on when you are changing jobs, because they are about gathering as much information as possible on an unfamiliar company or industry. These informal conversations can lead to an actual job down the road or to a reference for an opening elsewhere. They are typically shorter than job interviews, which can last anywhere between an hour and ninety minutes. You will probably be the one to initiate the meeting, which can take place at the work site or off-site in a less formal setting like a coffee shop or restaurant. If you are going out to eat or for drinks, always pick up the check!

One-on-one interviews are face-to-face meetings with a human resources rep or the manager of the department in which you are applying for a job. The purpose is for you to get to know each other and share information. This is your opportunity to share your qualifications for the job or project and to let the employer know why you are the best possible candidate.

Panel interviews involve more than one person conducting the questioning. These interviews are usually for more senior positions such as director or vice president. Often, a human resources representative is present.

Common Interview Mistakes

The following is a list of gaffes that people frequently make before, during, and after an interview. Avoiding these self-sabotaging mistakes will help you to get that job you want.

▶ **Being unprepared.** Not doing your homework about the company you are interviewing with before an interview is grounds for instant elimination as a candidate.

Quick-fix change: Most companies have websites, so it takes little time or effort to do research on the Internet. If you don't own a computer, use one at your local library. If there are trade magazines for the industry you are interested in, read some of the latest issues to get the most up-to-date information about what's going on in the field. You can use a headline for one of the questions you ask the interviewer or as a topic of conversation. For example, you might say, "I just read in *Medical Marketing News* that the FDA is close to approving one of the drugs your company is pitching. Do you have a full team working on that account?"

▶ **Not knowing why you are a good candidate for the job.** One of the first questions you will be asked, after the interviewer goes over your résumé, is why you think you are a good candidate for the job.

Quick-fix change: Practice your answer to this question before you go on the interview. If you can, come up with three reasons why you are the *best* candidate for the job.

▶ **Nervousness.** Nearly everyone feels anxious during interviews, so a bit of nerves is expected. But having a bad case of the jitters can trip you up during interviews by making you stutter or blank out when asked a question, or by giving you sweaty palms or shaky hands.

Quick-fix change: If you get the flop sweats at interviews, make sure to wear a jacket or blazer to cover your perspiration. You should also arrive extra early to the interview, so you have time to go to the rest room and compose yourself. Go into a stall, and take five deep breaths to slow down your heart and racing mind. Do not drink caffeine before the interview; it will worsen the shakes and stutters. One technique I use when nervous is to do a silent scream in a rest room stall. Pretend you are underwater, and let out the tension without making a sound. It works for me!

▶ **Monopolizing the conversation.** While the interviewer is eager to hear your thoughts, be careful not to interrupt too often or monopolize the conversation.

Quick-fix change: Allowing the other person time to speak not only is respectful, but also will give you time to think about what you are going to say next. In addition, it provides fodder for questions about the position you are interested in. It's OK to pause once in a while and let your words sink in.

▶ **Giving one-word answers.** Being too reticent during an interview will make you appear like a new car that has run out of gas. One-word answers leave gaps of silence, which are uncomfortable for both parties.

Quick-fix change: The only way your interviewer can get a fix on you, other than by reading your résumé, is by hearing what you have to say and how you say it, so speak in full sentences. You can always repeat the question if you need some extra time to gather your thoughts.

▶ **Lying.** Not answering an interviewer's question by skirting the topic, rambling, or being vague is a red flag for employers.

Quick-fix change: Don't try to fudge your way through a difficult question. Say, "I'm not familiar with this subject." (See my interview prep sheet later in this chapter.)

▶ **Showing little enthusiasm for the job.** I can't tell you how many employers have complained to me about candidates who sleepwalk through their interview. Employers want to know that a candidate is excited about a job and will be happy coming to work each day.

Quick-fix change: If you are going for a job that you really want, show it in your voice and demeanor. Let the employer know your interest by saying straight out that you are impressed with the company and would be excited to work there. Enthusiasm will often trump experience when all else is equal.

▶ **Being too modest.** Job interviews are not the place for modesty. They are a time to trumpet your successes and to let employers know why you are good at what you do.

Quick-fix change: Go over your past job triumphs before your interview, so they are fresh in your mind. Bring a portfolio of your work with you, if you have documents that back up your triumphs, and do a show-and-tell. Make sure to include how your work helped the company's bottom line, if applicable.

▶ **Poor appearance and body language.** I've written entire chapters on both, so if you've read Chapters 2 and 6, you should know what to do if these are issues for you.

Quick-fix change: Dress appropriately for the industry you are interviewing for. Don't slouch. Make eye contact, and be open and friendly in your demeanor, which means smiling and keeping your arms uncrossed.

▶ **Not understanding all aspects of the job.** Frequently, people interview for jobs they are unqualified for. Then they are blindsided when an interviewer asks about skills they don't have.

Quick-fix change: Make sure to do the proper research on the job you are going for, so you know exactly what skills are involved.

▶ **Bad-mouthing a former employer.** It's a small world, so you never know if your former boss is friends with your interviewer. If you rant about your current or former job, the interviewer will conclude that you'll do the same thing if this position doesn't work out.

Quick-fix change: No matter how bad your current or former employer was, resist the temptation to vent during your interview. If asked why you want to move, say you are looking for new challenges, and keep it at that.

▶ **Being defensive.** If your interviewer throws you a curveball by bringing up something negative that happened to you in the past, try not to react defensively.

Quick-fix change: Look at these difficult questions as an opportunity to put a good spin on a bad experience, so talk about what you learned from it and how it helped you grow as a professional.

▶ ANNA'S TIPS FOR SUCCESSFUL INTERVIEWING ▶▶

- ▶ Prepare yourself by doing research in advance.
- ▶ Dress appropriately for the position.
- ▶ Treat each interview as an opportunity to get to know the employer.
- ▶ Approach each interview as a chance to advance your career.
- ▶ Keep an open mind about what others have told you about the company.
- ▶ Don't live in the past. Even if you were not successful in a previous interview, you still might succeed in the next one.

Continued

- ▶ Always be yourself. If you are turned down for a job based on personality differences, it's not the right job for you.
- ▶ Don't be modest; sell yourself by preparing two success stories to tell.
- ▶ Have a good opening statement about yourself.
- ▶ Link your previous experience with what's needed for the job.
- ▶ Turn negative experiences into a positive by figuring out what you learned from them.
- ▶ Make eye contact, and have a strong handshake.
- ▶ Match the energy of the interviewer.
- ▶ Stay calm if the interview isn't going well; there will be others.
- ▶ Avoid personal details that are irrelevant to the position.
- ▶ Maintain a positive attitude.
- ▶ Record a video of yourself being interviewed. This will help you fix any negative body language and facial expressions. It will also help you tamp down any nervous energy or ramp up your enthusiasm if your energy level is low.

The Salary Question

Asking about salary is one of the most difficult parts of the interview process. Most people are uncomfortable talking about money, and it is a sensitive issue for employers as well, especially in bad economic times. Try to keep in mind that your self-worth is not connected to your net worth, so if you are not making as much as you think you deserve, it doesn't mean you are less valuable as a person.

Be prepared to answer the question of how much you currently make, because this figure will be the basis for how much you will be offered. Try to avoid this question, if possible, by saying you are making a salary compatible with your title and experience. If pressed, round up to the nearest high figure, but say that you are looking to go up a pay grade in your new job.

In the following situations, you can expect that your salary history will be requested during the interview process. For each situation, I've suggested ways to respond:

▶ **Applications.** If your application requests a salary history, you can either ignore that section or write that you would like to discuss salary in person, so you get to the next step of a face-to-face interview. In some instances, however, you will not be considered unless you provide your current salary. But if your background is a perfect fit for the job you are applying for, oftentimes the employer will ignore the request on the application and call you in for an interview.

▶ **Interviewer questions.** If an interviewer asks how much you are looking for, try to delay the discussion of salary as long as possible, or keep your answer vague, such as "My total compensation package was in the low six figures." If you must answer directly, give a range instead of a solid figure: "Somewhere between $50,000 and $70,000," with the low figure being an amount that is acceptable to you. If the salary offered is below what you want, be ready to walk away from the offer if you intend to negotiate for a higher salary. If you really want or need the job, say something like, "My compensation is not as important as my finding a good fit," or, "That would work, if there are possible bonuses and six-month salary reviews." If the hiring manager really wants you, he or she will find a way to sweeten the pot so you will take the job.

▶ **Recruiter questions.** If you are working with a recruiter, this person is likely to ask what you are looking for. It is in the recruiter's best interest for you to make as much as possible, because the recruiter will take a percentage of your annual salary at the new job as a fee. That said, it is also important to recruiters not to offer a candidate who will then turn around and refuse the job because of a salary dispute. You must be honest with a head-hunter about your minimum salary requirements.

Your Interview Preparation Worksheet

Fill out the following questionnaire before your next interview, so you will be prepared if these questions arise:

What are your qualifications for the job, including your educational background? _____

_____

_____

_____

_____

_____

What job skills do you have that will help in this position?

_____

_____

_____

_____

_____

_____

Describe some of your professional success stories.

_____

_____

_____

_____

_____

_____

How would you describe your personality and character?

_____

_____

_____

_____

_____

_____

What are some of your outside interests?

_____

_____

_____

_____

_____

_____

What are your strengths? _____

_____

_____

_____

_____

_____

What are your weaknesses? _____

_____

_____

_____

_____

_____

Why should we hire you? _____

_____

_____

_____

_____

_____

What decision did you make in the past year that you are proud of? Why? _____

_____

_____

_____

_____

_____

What decision did you make in the past year that you wish you could change? Why? _____

_____

_____

_____

_____

_____

Give an example of a time when you managed a conflict with a coworker. _____

_____

_____

_____

_____

_____

_____

Describe a current project you are working on and how it is going. _____

_____

_____

_____

_____

_____

Why do you want to leave your current job? _____

_____

_____

_____

_____

What are your salary requirements? _____

▶ **INTERVIEW PREPARATION CHECKLIST** ▶▶▶

Use this quick prep checklist before going on your next interview:

- ☐ I researched the job opening, including details of the main duties and what the manager is looking for.
- ☐ I developed a strategy for the interview, and I know the name and proper spelling of the person I will be meeting.
- ☐ I have made a list of my qualifications that make me the best candidate for the job.
- ☐ I know at least two success stories that will convey my qualifications.
- ☐ I've practiced my introduction and my success stories.
- ☐ I have a list of questions to ask the interviewer.
- ☐ I have spoken to someone who can give me information about the position I'm applying for.
- ☐ My interview outfit is ready to wear and in mint condition.
- ☐ I know how to get to my interview.

Interview Survival Kit

Bring the following items with you to the interview:

▶ Breath mints

▶ Extra shirt or blouse (in case you spill something or sweat too much). This should be in your car or at your hotel nearby, or you can hang it in the coat closet in the waiting room.

▶ Extra pair of hose (if you are wearing a skirt)

▶ Comb, brush, and makeup

Making a Short Presentation

Sometimes you will be asked to make a short presentation if the position you seek requires you to do public speaking, sales, or pitching to potential clients. The following checklists will help you to prepare for a knockout presentation:

Planning

▶ Arrange your material in the order in which you will be presenting it.

▶ Explain your three key points.

Rehearsing

Practice what you want to say out loud until you are comfortable with expressing your key points and timing. Practice in front of:

▶ A mirror or video recorder, so you know how you look.

▶ Friends or relatives. Ask for feedback, both positive and negative.

▶ A clock or timer, so you stay within your allotted time limit.

Presenting

If you are using visual aids, don't let them upstage you—it's you doing the talking, not the visual aids. Do remember to:

▶ Engage the audience by making eye contact.

▶ Stand up when giving your presentation.

▶ Keep your message simple and direct.

▶ Use handouts to illustrate your points, if applicable.

▶ Try to relax and have fun by injecting humor into the presentation, if appropriate.

Dressing Mistakes to Avoid at an Interview

Some general rules define what to wear at an interview. A good starting point is that whenever you are in doubt, you should err on the more conservative side. Despite the differences in various regions (for example, New York is more formal, and California more laid-back) and the variety of corporate cultures based on industries (financial and legal are more conservative, while advertising, technology, and publishing are more informal), the professional wardrobe has begun to strike a happy medium.

Interview clothes can reveal a bit about who you are or aspire to be, but they should not stand out by being unusual or quirky. Remember, the interviewer is more interested in what you are saying than what you are wearing, so you want him or her to focus on you, not your clothes. This is not the time to make a fashion statement. Here are common wardrobe faux pas to avoid when you are going on an interview:

- ▶ **Wild nail polish.** Extremely long nails are a turnoff, as are decals or wild-colored nail polish. Stick with clear, light pink or subdued red. Men should get a manicure before an interview so their nails look cut and polished.
- ▶ **Jewelry that jangles.** Don't wear more than two rings on one hand or more than one earring per ear. Absolutely no face jewelry or ankle bracelets are appropriate for interviews.
- ▶ **Open-toe shoes, backless shoes, or stilettos.** Make sure your shoes are closed and that the heel is no higher than two inches. Your shoes should be in great condition and up-to-date in terms of style.

- ▶ **Bare legs.** Most women hate pantyhose, but I'm afraid we must wear them on an interview, even if our legs are tan and even if the weather is hot. Stockings should be neutral colors or match your shoes—no fishnets or seams.
- ▶ **Out-of-date suits.** Suits with lapels that are too wide (three inches or more) or too narrow (one inch or less) should be retired. If you don't want to get rid of them, a good tailor can alter the lapels for you.
- ▶ **Short skirts.** If you're wearing a skirt, your hem should not be more than three inches above the knee. Do not wear capri pants or leggings to an interview.
- ▶ **Leather jackets.** Save the leather for your leisure time.
- ▶ **Short-sleeved shirts.** Interview shirts should always have long sleeves and a collar. No turtlenecks, please.
- ▶ **Printed or trendy handbags.** Purses, like your dress, should be conservative and inconspicuous. Interviews are not the time to show off your $2,000 purple Fendi.
- ▶ **Red briefcases.** Briefcases also should be conservative in color and always in top condition. Stick to black or brown leather.
- ▶ **Carrying a backpack or fanny pack.** These kinds of totes are meant for casual places like the gym, school, or travel.
- ▶ **Wearing your sunglasses on your head.** Take your sunglasses off when you arrive, and put them in a case, not on your head or folded on your shirt. Unless you're Anna Wintour or Jack Nicholson, never wear sunglasses indoors.
- ▶ **A cheesy tie.** Ties should be made of silk, no less than three and a quarter inches wide, with a conservative pattern that complements the color of your dress shirt. Powerful colors include red and burgundy.
- ▶ **Overly bright or patterned clothing.** Keep it simple, and no stripes or flowers!

- ▶ **Too much makeup.** Wear a neutral-color lipstick and no eye shadow or false lashes.
- ▶ **Unnatural hair color or comb-overs.** Women should make sure their hair has been recently styled. Men who are bald or have a receding hairline should shave their hair close to the head, rather than comb it over. Never, ever wear a toupee!
- ▶ **Too much perfume or aftershave.** Your interviewer should not smell you before and after you leave a room. Some people are allergic to fragrances; if you must wear one, make sure it is subtle.
- ▶ **Belts and shoes that don't match.** Your belt and shoes should always be made of leather and match in color. The best colors for men are black or cordovan.
- ▶ **Tags on your clothes.** It's great to wear a new suit or outfit to an interview, but don't forget to take the tags off. Likewise, remove all extra buttons, and remember to cut the zigzag thread that keeps pockets and slits closed.
- ▶ **Stains.** Check your clothing for stains several days before your interview, so you have time to get them cleaned.

Sample Interview Questions (Practice Test)

Before your next interview, ask yourself (or get a friend to ask you) the following frequently asked interview questions, so you will be prepared with your best possible answers.

- ▶ Tell me about yourself.
- ▶ Why did you leave your last job?

- ▶ Do you know anything about our company?
- ▶ What did you like about your last job?
- ▶ What would you like to be doing five years from now?
- ▶ Can you work under pressure?
- ▶ Could you describe a difficult problem and how you dealt with it?
- ▶ Why do you want to work here?
- ▶ What were some of the things you did not like about your last job?
- ▶ What do you consider your most significant weaknesses?
- ▶ What are your biggest accomplishments?
- ▶ How do you accept criticism?
- ▶ What is the most difficult situation you have faced?
- ▶ What are some of the things that bother you?
- ▶ What do you consider your most significant strengths?
- ▶ Do you prefer working with others or alone?
- ▶ How do you get along with different types of people?
- ▶ Can you give me an example of a project that didn't work out well?
- ▶ What are some of the things you and your supervisor have disagreed on?

Ten Questions to Ask the Interviewer

Most interviewers will allow the applicant to ask questions about the company or job he or she is applying for, so be prepared with at least one or two questions. Here are some suggestions:

- ▶ How would you describe the duties of this job?
- ▶ What are some of the biggest challenges of this position?

- ▶ What do you like best about working at this company?
- ▶ What are some of your company's goals for the future?
- ▶ How would you describe the ideal candidate for this job?
- ▶ How would you describe the corporate culture here?
- ▶ Why did the person I would be replacing leave?
- ▶ May I talk to the person who had this job before me?
- ▶ What are the opportunities for growth in this position?
- ▶ Is there anything else I can tell you about my qualifications?

The Follow-Up

It is imperative that you follow up with a thank-you note by letter or e-mail within two days after an interview. The note serves several purposes:

- ▶ Showing appreciation for the employer's time and interest
- ▶ Reiterating your interest in and enthusiasm about the organization and position
- ▶ Providing information you forgot to mention during your interview
- ▶ Following up with any information the employer might have asked you to provide

If more than a week has passed since you were told you would hear something from the employer about a decision, call or e-mail to inquire about the status of the position. A polite inquiry shows that you are still interested, and it might prompt the interviewer to make a decision or schedule additional interviews with others in the company, if necessary.

Sample Follow-Up Letter

Here is an example of a good, basic follow-up thank-you letter. Use this as a guide, and add your own personal touches:

> Thank you again for the opportunity to meet with you. I enjoyed learning more about [*company name*], and the interview has confirmed my strong interest in becoming a part of your team. As I mentioned, the position described sounds like an excellent fit with my skills and experience. Please let me know if I can supply you with any more information about my qualifications. I look forward to hearing about the next step to this process.
>
> Cordially,
>
> Your name
> Address
> Phone numbers
> E-mail
> Website (if any)

Your CV is Your Calling Card: Change One Thing About Your Résumé

In troubled economic times, it is even more important to have a sterling résumé. Look at other people's résumés in your chosen field to find a style and format you like best. If necessary, get a professional editor to help write and format your curriculum vitae (CV). The paper stock is less important than what's on the paper, so don't waste your money on expensive paper.

If you aren't sure whether your résumé is ready for circulation, take the following quiz to find out:

Does your résumé have an objective statement?

1. I'm trying to keep my options open, so my résumé has a general objective statement that doesn't tie me to any one position.
2. My résumé doesn't have an objective statement.
3. My résumé is targeted to my current career goal.

Answer: 3. The most effective résumés have an objective or summary that includes a clear job target. This helps employers know immediately what your career goals are without digging through the résumé.

Does your résumé have keywords that apply to your industry?

1. My field has a lot of industry jargon, which I added to my résumé.
2. I didn't think about adding keywords. I wrote my résumé and hoped for the best.
3. I've incorporated industry buzzwords and skills that I know apply to my career goal.

Answer: 3. There is a difference between trite jargon and buzzwords that might get your résumé pulled in an online applicant search by a recruiter. Examples of key buzzwords are job titles (sales manager, project manager, network administrator), specific skills (HTML, project management, financial analysis), and education (M.B.A., B.A., B.S.). Examples of business jargon are *return on investment, interface, takeaway, face time,* and *knowledge transfer.*

Does your résumé contain specifics about your accomplishments?

1. Yes, my résumé contains specific examples of how my employers benefited from my performance. Wherever possible, I have included measurable outcomes of my work.
2. No, I can talk about that in the job interview.
3. No, I haven't included accomplishments on my résumé.

Answer: 1. The résumé is a great place to put your accomplishments, and the more specific, the better. While you don't need to explain your accomplishments in great detail, you should give specific, quantifiable examples of how you benefited your employers. What problems or challenges did you face? What actions did you take to overcome the problems? Keep in mind that most companies value employees who increase profits, improve service, enhance efficiency, and save money.

Have you included personal information such as age, marital status, and hobbies?

1. Yes, I would like employers to know a little about my personal life.
2. No, I haven't included personal information, but I added a list of hobbies.
3. No, I haven't included any personal information on my résumé.

Answer: 3. Your résumé should not include personal information such as height, weight, age, hobbies, or marital status. Not only is this information irrelevant (who cares if you're a fly fisher?), it is illegal to ask if you are married or single during a job interview or to use the fact that you have kids as a criterion for a hiring decision.

Is your résumé tailored to the job you are looking for?

1. Yes, I use several different résumés depending on what job I'm applying for.
2. No, I have only one résumé that I use for all job applications.
3. My résumé is the same, but I change my job objective depending on the position I'm going for.

Answers: 1 and 3. It is OK to have more than one résumé depending on where you are applying. Some experience is more important than others to certain industries, and your creative-writing teaching experience won't be relevant for an accounting job, so you can leave that out when targeting the financial industry.

Do you use the personal pronouns *I*, *me*, and *my* in your résumé?

1. Yes, I have used *I*, *me*, and *my* throughout my résumé.
2. No, there are no personal pronouns in my résumé.
3. I have used the words *I* and *my* in the objective statement only.

Answer: 2. There is no need to use personal pronouns in your résumé, because it is assumed that you are writing about yourself. The same goes for your job objective.

How would you describe your ideal company on your résumé?

1. It would be a job with excellent benefits, flextime, salary, and bonuses.

2. It would be a company with potential for growth and advancement.

3. My ideal employer would benefit from my experience, skills, and qualifications.

Answer: 3. While all of the above would make for an ideal job, the best answer for your résumé would be one in which the employer benefits by bringing you aboard.

Does your résumé contain typos or grammatical errors?

1. I ran the spell-checker, and nothing came up.

2. I've sent out my résumé, and no one has commented about an error.

3. I read my résumé over carefully and gave it to several other people to proof for errors.

Answer: 3. It is not enough to spell-check, because the computer doesn't always catch mistakes. The same goes for feedback from people to whom you have sent your résumé. Most employers or human resources representatives won't bother to tell you about mistakes; they simply won't call you in for an interview. It's best to give your résumé to several people to proofread, especially if one of them is a professional writer or editor.

How effective is your current résumé?

1. I've sent my résumé to targeted employers, posted it online, and given it to recruiters and to people in my networking circle.

2. I've sent it out to hundreds of places, but I haven't heard back yet.

3. I've sent my résumé to targeted employers only.

Answer: 1. It's not enough to blanket the world with your résumé, even a well-crafted one. If you haven't heard back after sending it out to numerous places, it's time to rethink and redo. The best use of a résumé is to send it to targeted employers, recruiters, or online job search sites.

If Your Résumé Includes Any of the Following Details, Change It Now

▶ Personal information like height, weight, hobbies, marital status, or children
▶ What you expect the company to do for you
▶ Lies
▶ Jargon
▶ Salary requirements
▶ High school education (unless this is the highest level of education you have reached)
▶ Unusual typeface or fonts

If Your Résumé Does Not *Include the Following Details, Change It Now*

▶ Contact information (including e-mail, phone numbers, website)
▶ Objective (what kind of position you are seeking)
▶ Education (must include years attended)
▶ Experience (professional background, staff or freelance jobs, years attended, city/state)
▶ Honors and awards (not your bowling trophy—professional only)
▶ Professional memberships
▶ Skills (can include computer programs and languages you speak fluently)

Cut-to-the-Chase Cover Letters

Keep in mind that human resource managers and recruiters get hundreds of letters seeking employment, so here are some ways to help your letter rise to the top of the pile:

▶ **Keep it short.** I'm talking about no more than a page, and preferably only a few paragraphs. People are too busy to slog through a long narrative.

▶ **Lose the "To Whom It Concerns."** This salutation has gone the way of the vinyl record. Use the person's name instead. If you don't know it, use the person's title, but it's best to personalize whenever possible. For more formal companies, use Mr. or Ms.; for less formal, use either the first name or both the first and last.

▶ **Forget phrases like *in regard to.*** Get to the point quickly: "This is a response to your job listing on Monster.com for an advertising copywriter."

▶ **Drop a referral name in the first line.** If someone suggested that you contact a particular person about a job and gave you permission to use his or her name, do it in the first line. Personal recommendations mean a lot.

POSTSCRIPT

Do You Feel Different?

▶▶ NOW THAT YOU have finished the book and have done some or all of the exercises, one of two things has undoubtedly happened: You either feel like a different person than you were before, or you have a better understanding of what you need to do to strengthen your image so that you can achieve the confidence and recognition you deserve. If you are afraid to make a change in your life, you are not alone. But during my career as an image consultant, I have found that the more committed a person is to change, the greater the rewards. I hope that after reading this book, you have stopped the excuses and the negative thinking that have been holding you back.

Even though a lot of my advice is about altering your outward style and behavior, the most important change you can make starts on the inside. It's about believing in yourself. It's about envisioning yourself as the person you want to be, or in the job you've always dreamed of having. Whether you needed to make a small change or a monumental one (or maybe multiple changes), you are doing the work that needs to be done. As Charles Darwin once said, "It is not the strongest of the species that survives, nor the most intelligent that survives. It is the one that is most adaptable to change." So good luck with your personal or professional evolution!

Please sign up for my monthly newsletter or contact me with questions by going to personalimagesinc.com. I want to hear how your transformation is going!

RECOMMENDED
READING

Blink, Malcolm Gladwell
Body Language, Julius Fast
Body Language in the Workplace, Julius Fast
Brag: The Art of Tooting Your Own Horn Without Blowing It,
    Peggy Klaus
Career Match, Shoya Zichy
Crucial Conversations: Tools for Talking When Stakes Are High,
    Kerry Patterson, Joseph Grenny, Ron McMillan, and Al
    Switzler
Dress Smart Men, Kim Johnson Gross and Jeff Stone
Dress Smart Women, Kim Johnson Gross and Jeff Stone
Emotional Intelligence, Daniel Goleman
The Etiquette Advantage in Business, Emily Post and Peter Post
Executive Charisma, D. A. Benton
*Gestures: The Do's and Taboos of Body Language Around the
    World*, Roger E. Axtell
How Not to Look Old, Charla Krupp
How to Say It, Rosalie Maggio

How to Win Friends and Influence People, Dale Carnegie
In Style: Secrets of Style, Editors of *In Style* Magazine
Looks: Why They Matter More than You Ever Imagined, Gordon
   L. Patzer, Ph.D.
Networking Magic, Rick Frishman
*Networlding: Building Relationships and Opportunities for
   Success,* Melissa Giovagnoli and Jocelyn Carter-Miller
The Platinum Rule, Tony Alessandra, Ph.D.
Plus Style, Suzan Nanfeldt
Power Etiquette, Dana May Casperson
*Say It Like Obama: The Power of Speaking with Purpose and
   Vision,* Shel Leanne and Shelly Leanne
The Seven Habits of Highly Effective People, Stephen R. Covey
Talking from 9 to 5, Deborah Tannen, Ph.D.
The Tipping Point, Malcolm Gladwell
The Twenty-One Irrefutable Laws of Leadership, John C.
   Maxwell
What Got You Here Won't Get You There, Marshall Goldsmith

CLOTHING AND ACCESSORY LISTS BY PRICE

MEN	WOMEN
▶ **Suits, jackets, and separates**	▶ **Suits, jackets, slacks, and skirts**
$200–$300	**$200–$300**
Chaps	Kasper
Dockers	Style & Co. (Macy's)
Haggar	NY Collection
Stafford (JCPenney)	Evan Picone
Merona (Target)	Michael Kors
	Kenneth Cole
	Worthington (JCPenney)
	Talbots
	Ann Taylor

MEN	WOMEN

▶ Suits

▶ Suits

$495–$900	**$495–$900**
Alfani (Macy's)	Anne Klein New York
Nautica	Lafayette 148
Calvin Klein	Hugo Boss Women's
Inc. International (Macy's)	Eileen Fisher
Ralph Lauren	Ellen Tracy
Tasso Elba	Classiques Entier (Nordstrom)
$700–$1,200	**$700–$1,200**
Hart Schaffner Marx	St. John Knits
Joseph Abboud	Armani Collezioni
Boss	Dana Buchman
$1,200–$3,500	**$1,200–$3,500**
Oxford	Donna Karan Collection
Hickey Freeman	Escada
Nicky Hilton	Burberry
Armani	Ralph Lauren Blue or
Burberry	Black Label
	Armani
$4,000 and up	**$4,000 and up**
Brioni	Versace

▶ Shirts

▶ Shirts and Blouses

$19.99–$39.99	**$19.99–$39.99**
Haggar	Worthington (JCPenney)
Arrow	H&M

Chaps
Croft and Barrow (Kohl's)
Stafford
Claiborne

Simply Vera
Croft and Barrow (Kohl's)
Chaps
Joseph A

$65–$125
Nordstrom Smartcare
Calvin Klein
Boss
Claiborne

$65–$125
NY Collection
Jones New York
Alfani (Macy's)
Ann Taylor
Talbots

$125–$250
Robert Graham
Versace
Boss
Burberry
Ben Sherman
John Varvatos

$125–$250
Eileen Fisher
Dana Buchman
Lafayette
Michael Kors
Calvin Klein
JS Collections

▶ **Shoes**

▶ **Shoes**

$50–$100
Rockport
Born
Bass
Dockers
Calvin Klein
Florsheim
Naturalizer
Bostonian
Clarks

$50–$100
Nine West
Vaneli
Me Too
Circa Joan & David
Clarks
Villager (Kohl's)
Simply Vera
Liz Claiborne
Naturalizer

MEN	WOMEN

▶**Shoes** ▶ **Shoes**

$100–$250

$100–$250	**$100–$250**
Cole Haan	Via Spiga
Johnston & Murphy	Bruno Magli
Kenneth Cole Reaction	Munro
Hampton (Nordstrom)	Soft Spot
ENZO Angiolini	

$250–$750	**$250–$500**
Allen-Edmonds	Paul Green
Cole Haan	Donald J. Pliner
Mezlen (Nordstrom)	Tanya Rose
Bruno Magli	Stuart Weitzman
Ferragamo	Ferragamo

▶ **Belts** ▶ **Belts**

$50–150	**$25–$150**
Nordstrom	Simply Vera
Dockers	Lauren by Ralph Lauren
Bass	Nordstrom
Boss	Brighton
Cole Haan	

$150 and up	**$150 and up**
Ferragamo	Ferragamo
John Varvatos	Michael Kors
Coach	Coach

BRIEFCASES (MEN AND WOMEN)

Tumi
Coach

STORES (MEN AND WOMEN)

▶ Discount

T. J. Maxx
Nordstrom Rack
Marshall's
Loehmann's

▶ Low Cost

Target
Kohl's

▶ Midrange

Macy's
Lord & Taylor
Dillard's

▶ Mid to High End

Nordstrom
Saks
Bloomingdales

STORES (MEN AND WOMEN)

▶ High End

Neiman Marcus
Barney's
Bergdorf Goodman

▶ Online Only

QVC.com
Overstock

INDEX